St. Mary's Catholic Cemetery, Arney, Cleenish Parish, County Fermanagh

by

David R. Elliott

Irish Genealogy Series

KinFolk Finders

© David R. Elliott, 2025

This book is not to be copied or put into electronic format without the expressed written permission of Kinfolk Finders.

David R. Elliott, Ph.D., M.Div., is a past-chair of the London & Middlesex Branch of the Ontario Genealogical Society and the founding vice-chair of the organization's Ireland Special Interest Group.

ISBN: 978-1-927357-78-1

Cover photo: St. Mary's Catholic Church and Section A of its cemetery. (DRE 2023).

Kinfolk Finders

154 Main Street, Parkhill,

Ontario, Canada   N0M 2K0

1-519-294-0728

Preface to the Irish Genealogy Series' New Format

When we first visited Ireland in 2004, we were searching for our Irish ancestors. We soon discovered that so many of its cemeteries had never been indexed. Those that had been done, were done poorly with only the most legible tombstones being recorded, and often the published indexes listed the stones alphabetically without any indication of their location or *in situ* context. Without detailed site maps, it was very difficult locating those stones. Taking our cue from the past cemetery indexing projects of the Ontario Genealogical Society, we felt that a better job could be done for Irish cemeteries.

The 1922 destruction of almost all of the pre-1901 Irish census records and the burning of most of the Church of Ireland (Anglican) parish registers, marriage bonds and wills in the explosion at the General Registry Office in Dublin during the civil war was a great tragedy. We are forced to use all sources available to us to recreate the past; information gained from cemeteries is thus very important.

Preface

With my background in archaeology, we have taken advantage of aerial photography and noting ground cover changes to detect buried stones, employing surveying techniques to map the cemeteries, using plain flour and water to highlight difficult texts, and creating digital photographic techniques to capture the images of hard-to-read inscriptions.

As a historian, I have sought to provide the most accurate reproduction of the information on the tombstones by checking questionable names, dates and ages against surviving parish registers, and civil registrations of births, marriages and deaths. In our transcriptions, we have provided the correct spellings of misspelled townlands, checking locations against the Tithe Applotments, the Griffith Valuation, and surviving census records. The name of the townland is so very important in Irish genealogical research.

In our research of each graveyard, we have keyed the transcriptions according to sections, rows and tombstone numbers to our maps of the cemeteries and their indexes. We have also recorded the spaces which may contain unmarked graves or unused plots. Every name on the tombstones has been recorded in the alphabetical comprehensive index at the back of each book.

Preface

In the transcriptions of tombstones section, we have employed various terms to describe the different types of grave markers. We have used the word plot to describe a defined burial area with four borders or different types of fences. Some have perimeter inscriptions on the curbs. Some types of plots have only one border extending across their width and supports the headstone. We have called these partial plots. Some plots have added fences; some plots are very elaborate.

There are various kinds of burial memorials found in the cemeteries. There are free-standing headstones, pedestal markers, temporary wooden crosses with plaques, flat stones, raised flats and sarcophagi (stone coffins above ground), also mausoleums and massive monuments. As well, sometimes there are memorials on the walls inside the churches which can provide additional genealogical information.

To help readers identify what we are describing, we have included a selection of different types tombstone styles that we have encountered across Ireland; in other words, a visual glossary.

Our own research and research for our clients has led us to index cemeteries in counties Antrim, Donegal, Fermanagh, Leitrim, Tyrone and also Wicklow. Initially

Preface

our company, KinFolk Finders, published our indexes in-house, but we are now publishing them in a new format produced by Lightning Source in order to facilitate wider international exposure and ease of access. Eventually, all of our previous titles will be put into this new format. Some smaller cemetery indexes will be consolidated with others in the same parish or pastoral charge.

For those who cannot personally visit these Irish cemeteries, we have put our photographs of each tombstone on FindmyPast.ie .

Table of Contents

Preface to the Irish Genealogy Series......................iii

Table of Contents..1

Introduction 3

Acknowledgements..7

Map of Counties in Ireland.................................9

Map of Parishes in County Fermanagh....................10

Map of Arney Area..11

Map of the St. Mary's Cemetery.........................12

Map of Section A..13

Map of Section B..14

Map of Section C..15

Map of Section E..16

Scenes of the Church and Cemetery.......................17

Bibliography.............................. 26

Tombstone styles 27

Transcriptions of Tombstones 49

Key to Index of Names................................100

Index of Names.. 101

Irish Genealogy Series Titles............................127

Introduction

St. Mary's Roman Catholic Church and its cemetery are located on the Arney Road (C438) west of Bellanaleck, on Mullymesker Townland near the hamlet of Arney. The church was built sometime after Catholic Emancipation in 1828. It was mentioned in the 1835 Ordnance Survey Memoirs and was then called Sessiagh Chapel, holding about 400 worshippers.[1] The oldest memorial in its cemetery dates from 1837.

Earlier Catholic burials may have taken place at the ruins of a 6th century monastery located at the north end of Cleenish Island in Upper Lough Erne, which had a graveyard. It was still being used in 1835, but there were no inscriptions on the tombstones.[2] Some of those graves

---

[1] Angélique Day and Patrick McWilliams, eds. *Ordnance Survey Memoirs of Ireland Volume 14: Parishes of Co. Fermanagh II, 1834-5* (Belfast: Institute of Irish Studies, Queen's University, 1992), p.17.

[2] *Ibid.*, p.20.

Introduction

were later moved to the Church of Ireland cemetery at Bellanaleck.[3]

Our interest in the Cleenish Island site began in 2015 after seeing some pictures of the site. We were able to find a large building block containing a three dimensional human face carved on it. That stone was mentioned in the 1835 Ordnance Survey report.[4]

(DRE 2015)

---

[3] David R. Elliott, *Bellanaleck Church of Ireland Cemetery* (Parkhill: Kinfolk Finders, 2011).

[4] Day and McWilliams, p.20.

Introduction

In September 2017 we had the pleasure of attending the official launch for *Making it Home*, a book about a group of Irish WWI veterans who were given land grants on the mainly uninhabited Cleenish Island.[5] Some of those Cleenish Island new residents belonged to St. Mary's Church.

Later that week we visited the St. Mary's cemetery to investigate it for our ongoing project of cemetery indexing. When Fiona Wright, one of the editors of the above mentioned book, heard of our plans to index St. Mary's cemetery she encouraged us to do so because they wanted to have more records for their local history project.

Because of other commitments and the intervention of Covid-19 we were not able to survey St. Mary's cemetery until 2023. The work was completed there on the 10th of June that year and reflects the known burials to that date.

As we transcribed the inscriptions on the tombstones, we found that sometimes the names of the townlands were spelled incorrectly. We have corrected

---

[5] Marion Maxwell and Fiona Wright, eds. *Making It Home: The resettlement of WWI ex-servicemen on Cleenish Island in Upper Lough Erne* (Bellanaleck: Bellanaleck Local History Group, 2017).

Introduction

them to conform to the standard names set in 1851. Where we have changed the spelling, we have indicated it with an asterisk.*

Because we are interested only in genealogical and historical information we have left out sayings, poems, scripture and supplications in our transcriptions unless they were necessary for grammatical sense.

We have plotted the rows on our map as best we could. There are a lot of green spaces which may contain unmarked graves.

Catholic cemeteries often contain important information on their tombstones about the social history of the area and the people buried in them. In this cemetery, you can find a celebration of a Republican who fought against the British at the Dublin Post Office in 1916 and also those who suffered during "the Troubles." One was a young woman murdered by a drunken British soldier in 1981. There was also a grave for a policeman killed in 1921 in a battle with the IRA.

Acknowledgements

David and Val Bailey of Blaney Caravan Park have continued to be our gracious hosts and encouragers of our genealogical endeavors in Fermanagh, since 2004. We are greatly indebted to Derek and Laura Elliott who loaned us their cottage from 2011 to 2017.

Blaney Caravan Park, our home away from home. (DRE 2019).

Acknowledgements

My friend David Keys, a military and police historian, caused me to take a closer look at one of the graves in this St. Mary's cemetery which belonged to a murdered policeman.

Special thanks goes to Brian Mitchell in Derry who granted permission for us to use and modify some of his parish maps from his *A New Genealogical Atlas of Ireland* published by Genealogical Publishing Co., Inc. in Baltimore.

Nancy Elliott prepared the maps displayed in this book. Linda Smith did copy editing of the text.

I must also thank various people who took time to talk to me while I was mapping and photographing the cemetery. They told me their stories about some of those buried there. One was Hugh Quigley. Another was one of the retired priests living at the Rectory next to the cemetery. He told me about his experiences during "the Troubles" while he was ministering at Belcoo in the western part of the parish.

Maps

The Counties of Ireland

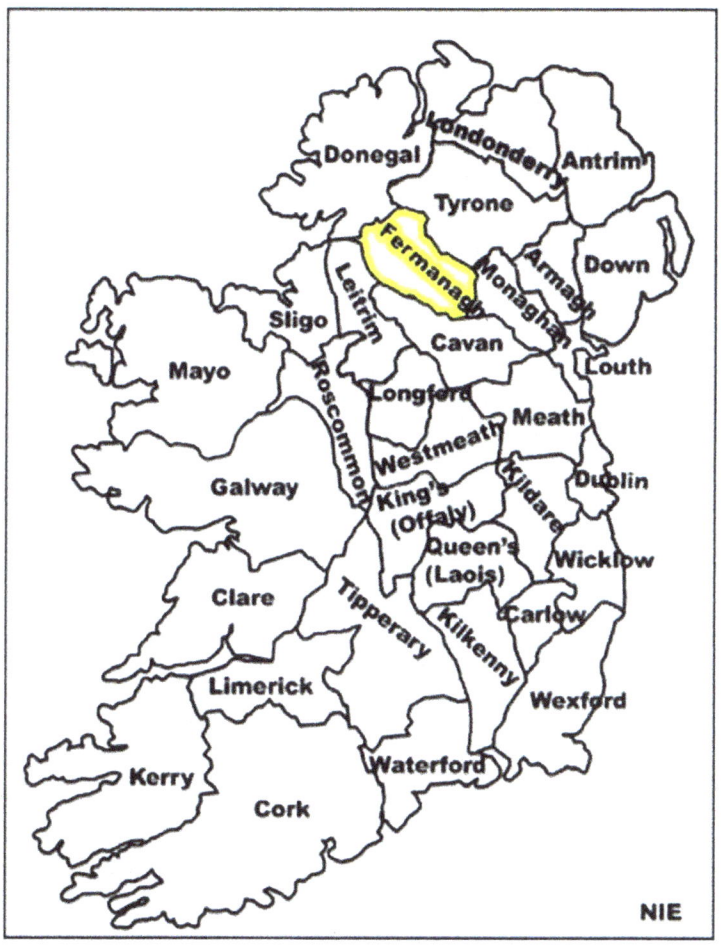

County Fermanagh highlighted. (NIE map 2012).

County Fermanagh Parishes

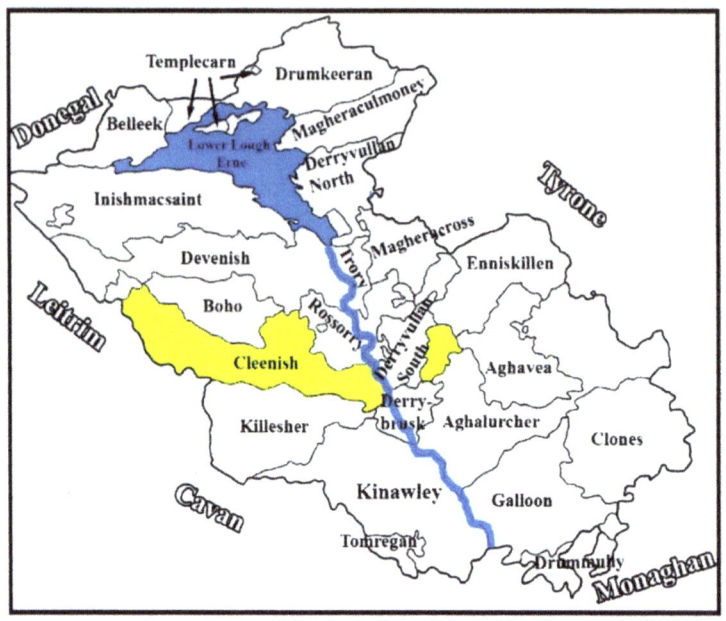

County Fermanagh parishes. Cleenish Parish highlighted. (NIE map 2024).

This is an approximate map of the parishes of County Fermanagh. It is very difficult to delineate the Upper Lough Erne on a map of this size because it is not a continuous large body of water, but a waterway interspersed with many islands. It is part of the Shannon River system that extends though the interior of Ireland. However, the Upper Lough Erne system becomes wider in places towards the southern border of the county. Cleenish Parish, featured in this book, is highlighted in yellow. It also has an eastern portion centered around Lisbellaw.

Maps

Location of the Cemetery

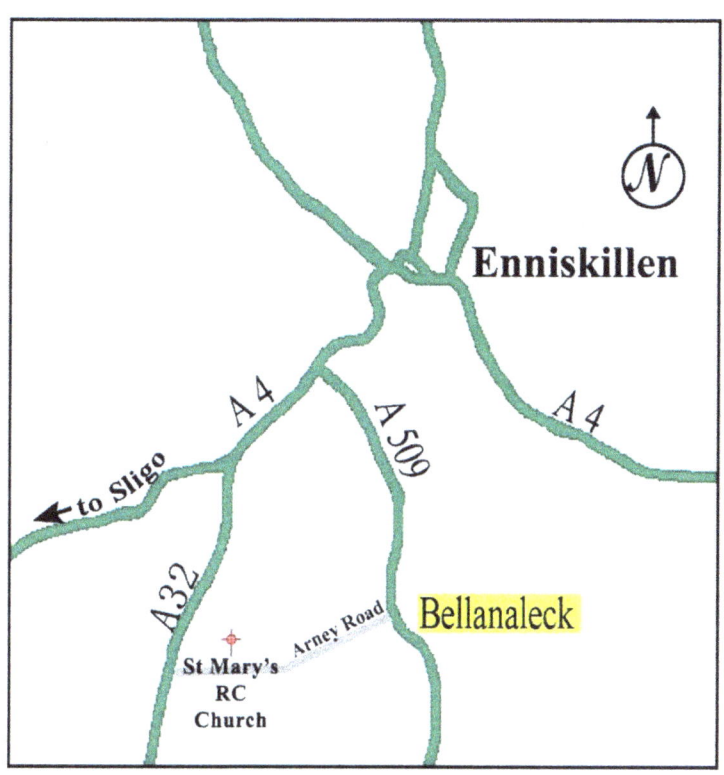

(NIE map 2025)

Maps

St. Mary's Cemetery Sections

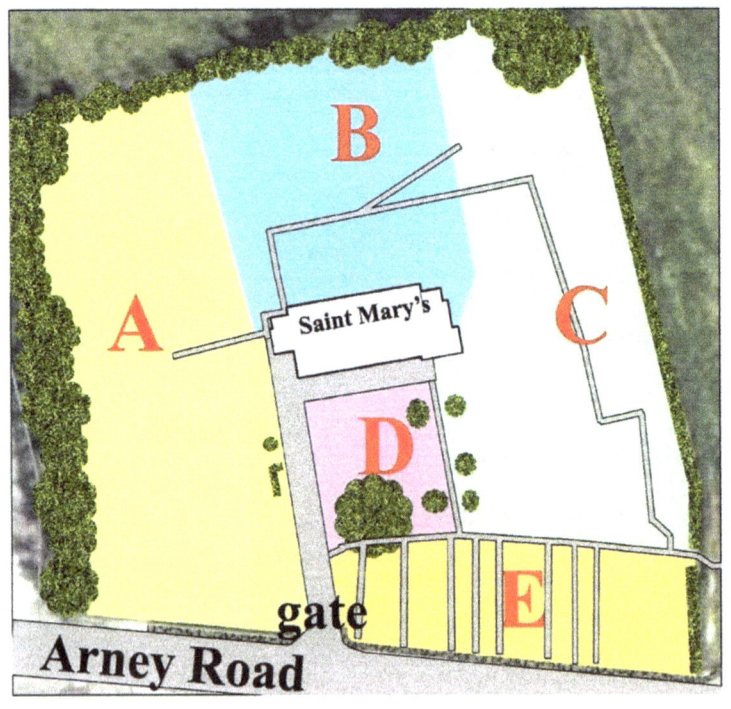

(NIE map 2025)

Section A

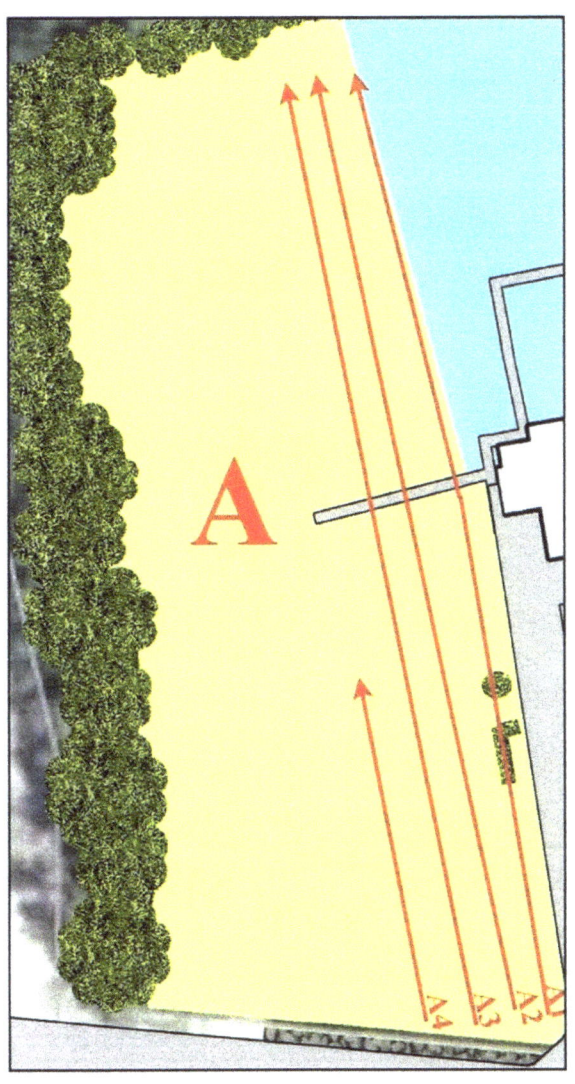

Rows occupied in 2023. (NIE map 2025)

Maps

Section B

(NIE map 2025)

Maps

Section C

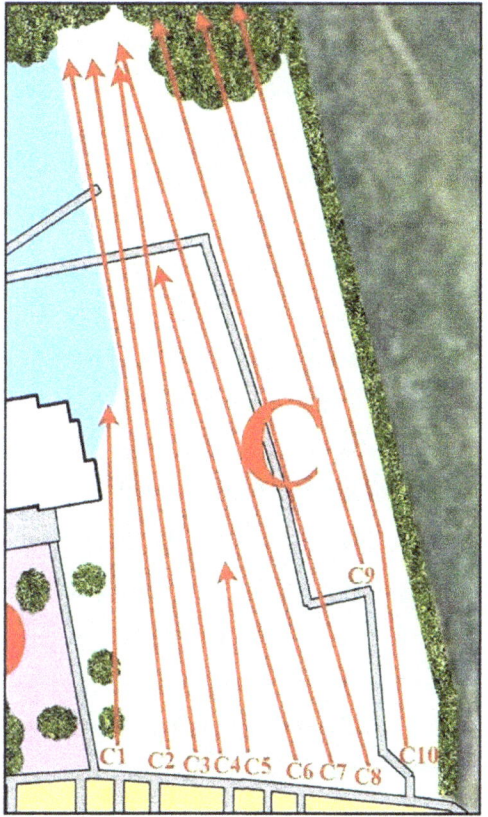

Irregular rows complicated the drafting of this map; the rows are approximate. (NIE map 2025).

SECTION E

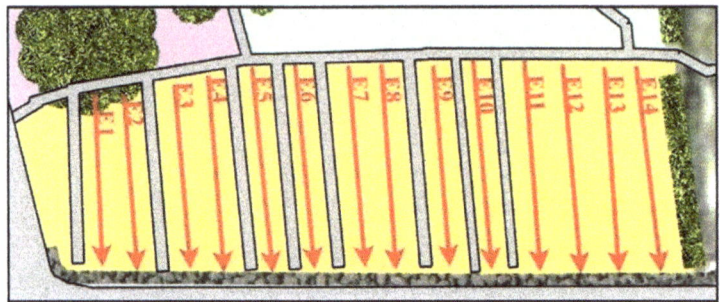

(NIE map 2023)

[Note: we have not supplied a map for Section D since there was only one row of priestly graves].

Scenes of the Church and Cemetery

St. Mary's Roman Catholic Church, Arney. South side. The row of Celtic crosses and tombstones to the right of church entrance (Section D) memorialized past parish priests. (DRE 2017).

Church interior. (DRE 2023).

Scenes of the Church and Cemetery

Section A. West side of church. (DRE 2023).

Scenes of the Church and Cemetery

Section B. North side of church. (DRE 2023).

Second C. East side of church. (DRE 2023).

Section D. South side of church. (DRE 2023).

Section E to the right of tree. Sidewalk to the left of tree leading to the Rectory. (DRE 2023).

Scenes of the Church and Cemetery

Section E has the highest density in this cemetery. (DRE 2023). Below, as seen from Arney Road. (DRE 2017).

C8-5. Smashed sarcophagus. It appears to be the oldest dated grave in the cemetery. The first reference is to a death in 1837. (DRE 2023).

Scenes of the Church and Cemetery

C9-4. Headstone tilted face down which was dangerously difficult to photograph. Picture taken of inscription while lying down and using a telephoto lense. The surface was also floured prior to taking the picture to enhance the text. (DRE 2023).

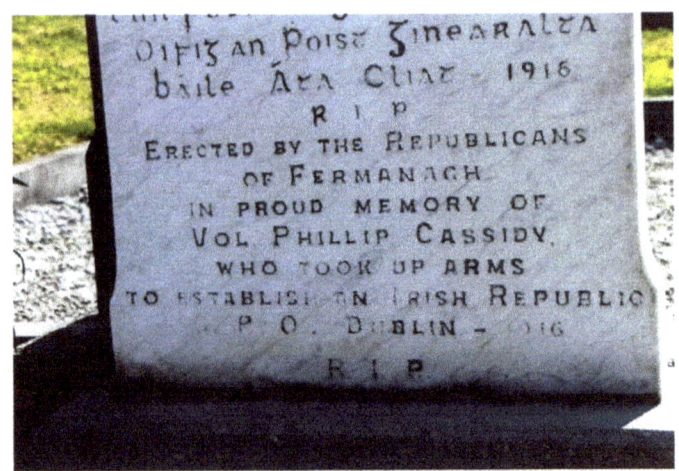

C3-3. Celebrating the 1916 Easter Uprising. In Gaelic with an English translation. (DRE 2023).

A2-3. Murdered young woman. (DRE 2023).

C-9-2. (DRE 2023). The civil registration of death reveals that Francis Creegan was a RIC sergeant who was shot and killed along with a number of other policeman 2nd June 1921 during a gun battle with members of the IRA in County Mayo.

Bibliography

Day, Angélique and Patrick McWilliams, eds. *Ordnance Survey Memoirs of Ireland Volume 14: Parishes of Co. Fermanagh II, 1834-5* Belfast: Institute of Irish Studies, Queen's University, 1992.

Elliott, David R. *Bellanaleck Church of Ireland Cemetery.* Parkhill: Kinfolk Finders, 2011.

Livingstone, Peader. *The Fermanagh Story.* Enniskillen: Cumann Seanchais Chlochair, St. Michael's College, 1969.

Maxwell, Marion and Fiona Wright, eds. *Making It Home: The resettlement of WWI ex-servicemen on Cleenish Island in Upper Lough Erne.* Bellanaleck: Bellanaleck Local History Group, 2017.

Mitchell, Brian. *A New Genealogical Atlas of Ireland*, 2nd edition. Baltimore: Genealogical Publishing Co., Inc., 2002.

Styles of Tombstones

Plots

Plot: a burial area with four defined borders. (Fivemiletown, DRE 2024).

A fenced plot with a pillar headstone with inscriptions on all four sides. (Monea, DRE 2006).

Tombstone Plates

Fenced plot with large funeral monument having architectural features. (Old Aghalurcher, DRE 2024).

Caged plot. (Monea, DRE 2023).

Partial plots with only one border, extending the full width of the burial area. (Colaghty, DRE 2023).

Tombstone Plates

Inscription on perimeter border of plot. (Derrbybrusk, DRE 2016).

Inscribed flower holder inside plot; sometimes containing genealogical data. (Tubrid, DRE 2016).

Some plots with large headstone also have large flagstone flat memorials which have become grassed over. The lettering is often very legible. (Monea, DRE 2006).

Flats

A large flat flagstone memorial from 1800. (Old Aghalurcher, DRE 2024).

Tombstone Plates

Crested flat stone with herald crest above memorial text. (Old Aghalurcher, DRE 2024).

Raised flat or table monument with an inscription. (Garrison, DRE 2008).

Types of Headstones

Simple free-standing headstone. Older ones often have sunk into the ground, burying the lower rows of the inscriptions. (Monea, DRE 2006).

Scroll-shaped headstones. (Derrybrusk, DRE 2016).

Military marker erected by the Commonwealth War Graves Commission. (Benmore, DRE 2007).

Tombstone Plates

Tree-shaped headstone. (Tubrid, DRE 2016).

Short decorative Celtic cross. (Breandrum, Enniskillen, DRE 2025).

Pedestal marker. (Garrison, DRE 2008).

Book-shaped pedestal marker. (Derrygonnelly, DRE 2009).

Tombstone Plates

With some fenced plots, instead of a headstone, an iron cast memorial plate was mounted on the railings. (Lisbellaw, DRE 2013).

Column funerary monument. (Clogher, DRE 2011).

High Celtic cross in a plot. (Ederney, DRE 2023).

Tombstone Plates

Stubby Celtic cross headstone. (Edenclaw, DRE 2023).

Small iron Celtic crosses. (Derrygonnelly, (DRE 2009).

Imitation Celtic cross headstone. These were common in the 17th and 18th centuries. (Aghavea, DRE 2012).

On the reverse side of the above stones were often symbols of death, with an eerie message: Skull, cross bones and a coffin. The bell (for whom the bell tolls; it tolls for thee) and the hourglass on its side (time has run out). (Aghavea, DRE 2012).

Tombstone Plates

Temporary wooden cross with plaque. (Belcoo, DRE 2015).

Roman cross headstone. (Edenclaw, DRE 2023).

Tombstone Plates

Stubby Roman cross headstone. (Brookborough, DRE 2019).

Tombstone Plates

Fancy children's burial markers in the shape of children's beds. (Fivemiletown, DRE 2011).

Children's plot with bench. (Fivemiletown, DRE 2024).

Sarcophagii

A sarcophagus is an above-ground stone coffin. (Benmore, DRE 2007).

Fancy low-profile sarcophagus. (Ballyshannon, DRE 2015).

Tombstone Plates

Mausoleums

Mausoleums can be large above-ground burial structures or large underground rooms for the burials of wealthy families as below. (Aghavea, DRE 2012).

Mausoleum. (Ardess, DRE 2019).

Memorial plaques inside churches can often supply information on family relationships, dates, and causes and places of death in distant places. (Banagher, County Offaly, DRE 2012).

Died at Madras, India, 1847. (Benmore, DRE 2008).

Transcriptions

SECTION A

Row A1

A1-1 [space].

A1-2 [**HUNT** plot]. In loving memory of **Helena McManus**, died 17th Oct. 1977. **Eugene Patrick Hunt** (33 Drumlin Heights, Enniskillen) died 5th October 1977. His wife **Mary Catherine** died 7th September 1983. Their son **Eugene** died 4th Feb. 2000. Their daughter **Maura** died 2nd Oct. 2017.

A1-3 [**McGOVERN** plot with stubby Celtic cross]. Sacred heart of Jesus have mercy on the soul of **Rose McGovern** (Sessiagh) who died 26th October 1967. Also her granddaughter **Mary Veronica** who died 21st October 1980, aged 31 years. Her husband **James** died 11th November 1996, aged 96 years. Her daughter **Rose Anne** who died 28th February 2014, aged 85 years.

A1-4 [Spaces and mounds. There is a vertical rock about one foot high which may have been a burial marker; no identification.]

A1-5 [Plot]. In loving memory of **Owen McTeggart**, died March 5th 1932, aged 54 years. Also his wife **Margaret** died Jan. 12th 1942, aged 72 years. Their daughter **Margaret** died Aug. 19th 1964.

A1-6 [**QUINN** plot with perimeter inscriptions]. **Sarah Quinn** died 29th May 1956, aged 80 yrs. **Hugh Quinn** died 19th Oct. 1966, aged 90 yrs. **Annie Eleanor** died 6th April 2010, aged 93 yrs.

A1-7 [**GOAN** plot with small Roman cross]. **Edward P. Goan**.

A1-8 [Large **COX** plot which extends into B2]. In loving memory. Pray for the soul of **Philip Cox** who died 28th March 1919, aged 77 years. And his wife **Ellen Cox** who died on 18th June 1922, aged 75 years. Also for the soul of **Mary Josephine Cox** who died 4th October 1930. Their son **Patrick** who died 27th Feb. 1967 and their son **John** who died 8th Sept. 1968. **John**'s wife **Alice** died 24th April 1988. **Jackie Cox** died 12th Nov. 2001. And his wife **Mary** died 4th July 2003.

A1-9 [**McCANN** partial plot with short Roman cross; no other identification].

A1-10 [spaces and mounds].

A1-11 [**SMYTH** plot]. In loving memory of **John Smyth** (Carneyhill*), died 1st August 1981. His wife **Frances** died 11th August 1986. Also the **Goan** Family (Carneyhill*).

A1-12 [space].

Transcriptions

[East-West walkway]

A1-13 [space and mounds].

A1-14 [Plot]. In memory of **Joseph Gunn** who died September 8th 1905, aged 11 years. Also our loving sister **Mary Jane** who died April 14th 1919, aged 22 years. Also our father **John Gunn** who died March 5th 1931, aged 80 years. And our mother **Rose Gunn** who died May 8th 1947, aged 93 years.

A1-15 [Plot]. In loving memory of the **Cooney** family (Sessiagh).

A1-16 [small space].

A1-17 [**GILHEANEY** plot with a perimeter inscription]. In loving memory of **James Gilheaney**, died 12th March 1952. His wife **Annie** died 29th June 1969, aged 82 years. Their son **Thomas** died 17th June 1946, aged 18 years. Their grandson **Thomas Maurice** died 28th March 1947, aged 8 months. Their son **Walter** died 15th April 1998, aged 76 years. His wife **Kathleen** died 21st February 2006, aged 90 years. [Perimeter]. Baby **Mairead Gilheaney** died October 1986.

A1-18 [spaces and mounds].

A1-19 [Plot with stubby Roman cross]. **Patrick McAuley** (Skea) died 18th October 1968, aged 87 years. Also his wife **Mary Ellen** died 15th April 1975, aged 84 years. Also her mother **Rose Gilligan** died 1918, aged 66 years. **Rose**'s

Transcriptions

son **James Gilligan** died 1920, aged 28 years. And her husband **Thomas** died 1922, aged 77 years. **John McAuley** died 5th November 2015, aged 95 years.

A1-20 [space].

A1-21 [**McCONNELL** plot]. In loving memory of **Bernard McConnell** (Tully), died 8th Dec. 1928, aged 68 yrs. His wife **Rose** died 25th Jan. 1950, aged 86 yrs. Their sons: **Thomas** died 15th Aug. 1959, aged 60 yrs. **Patrick** died 15th Dec. 1972, aged 76 yrs. Their daughter **Lizzy** died 6th Oct. 1987, aged 81 yrs.

A1-22 [space].

A1-23 [**JUDGE** plot sitting between Rows A1 and A2]. In loving memory of **Patrick Judge** (Derriens East), died 8th March 1990, aged 78 years. His wife **Eileen** died 30th Nov. 1995, aged 70 years. **Mary Ellen Power** died 7th Aug. 2019, aged 80 years.

ROW A2

A2-1 [**McTEGGART** plot]. In loving memory of **Thomas McTeggart** (Old Henry Street, Enniskillen) died 5th Aug. 1985. His wife **Emily** died 27th March 1995.

A2-2 [**FARMER** plot]. In loving memory of **Patrick Farmer** (35 Old Henry Street, Enniskillen), died 20th Jan. 1973. His wife **Mary** died 13th January 1984.

Transcriptions

A2-3 [**D'ARCY** plot]. In loving memory of our son **John Anthony D'Arcy** who died 18th August 1972, aged 26 years. His father **Thomas D'Arcy** who died 17th Feb. 1975. His sister **Angela** murdered by a British soldier 25th Nov. 1981, aged 24 years. His mother **Josephine D'Arcy** who died 27th July 2011, aged 92 years.

A2-4 [Plot]. In memory of **Frank** and **Margaret Quinn** (*nee* **Cassidy**).

A2-5 [spaces and mounds to large A1-8 plot which intrudes into A2].

A2-6 [space and mounds].

A2-7 [**D'ARCY** plot with headstone and plaque]. In loving memory of the **D'Arcy** family (Bellanaleck). [Plaque]. Treasured memories of **Gabriel D'Arcy**, a loving husband, father and grandfather, died 12th October 2011, aged 70 years.

A2-8 [**OWENS** plot]. In memory of **Jamesie**, **Annie** and **Cassie**.

A2-9 [Short white decorative Celtic cross]. In loving memory of **Mary Anne** and **James John Lilly** (Sligo Road).

A2-10 [space].

A2-11 [**SLEVIN** plot]. In loving memory of **Hugh Slevin**, died 10th Oct. 1923. His wife **Catherine** died 10th March 1950. Their daughter **Susan** died 10th May 1927. Their sons: **Joseph** died 21st June 1948. **Hugh** died 25th Dec. 1983.

[East-West walkway]

A2-12 [spaces and mounds].

A2-13 [**McCONNELL** flower holder with small Celtic cross].

A2-14 [spaces and mounds].

A2-15 [Headstone with lead letters missing]. In loving memory of our dear mother **Mary McCardle**, wife of **John McCardle**, died 11th Jan. 1887, aged 50 years. Also his daughter **Margaret Jane**, died Jan. 1891, aged 27 years.

A2-16 [**LUCY** plot]. In loving memory of **Anna Elizabeth**, born 12th June 1942, died 12 May 1944. **William Lucy** died 29th December 2000, aged 81 years. **Mary Lucy** died 24th October 2014, aged 94 yrs. **Frederick John Lucy (Freddie)** died 16th Dec. 2021, aged 69 yrs.

A2-17 [**McALOON** plot]. In loving memory of **Thomas McAloon**, died 10th Nov.1962, aged 74 years. And his loving wife **Margaret** died 13th Sept. 1989, aged 83 years. His son **Sean** died 18th June 2000, aged 75 years. His daughter **Rose Philomena Parr** died 5th June 2009, aged 75 years.

Transcriptions

A2-18 [Two stones, possibly part of a cross; no identification].

A2-19 [spaces and mounds].

A2-20 [Plot with stubby Celtic cross]. In loving memory of **Francis McNamara** (Corraglass*), died 17 Feb. 1978. His wife **Mary Elizabeth** died 5 July 1995. **Joseph Graham** died 20 June 1972. Their son **Gabriel (Gaby)** died 30 March 2008. **Bridget (Birdie) Graham** died 25 February 2010.

A2-21 [O'PREY plot]. In loving memory of **Patrick O'Prey**, died 1st April 1945. His wife **Delia** died 13th Feb. 1972. Their son Fr. **Thomas Patrick O'Prey** died 10th May 2002. Also the **Curry** family.

A2-22 [space].

A2-23 [Stubby Celtic cross with lead letters]. Erected by **Mary A. McGoldbrick** in memory of her husband **Peter McGoldbrick**, died 31st Jan. 1927, aged 68 yrs. Also her father **John Brady** died 10th April 1889, aged 72 yrs. Her mother **Catherine Brady** died 10th June 1920, aged 82 years. Her brother-in-law **Hugh McGoldbrick** died 26th Dec. 1923, aged 73 years.

A2-24 [Base and shaft of cross; no identification].

Transcriptions

ROW A3

A3-1 [**QUINN** plot]. In loving memory of **Kathleen Quinn** (43 Hillview Park), died 4th June 1985, aged 68 yrs. Her husband **Frank** died 11th January 1991, aged 82 years.

A3-2 [space].

A3-3 [Plot with short white decorative Celtic cross and plaque; no identification. The lettering on the plaque was too faint for us to be able to detect any names but appears to be a tribute to grandparents.]

A3-4 [**WOODCOCK** plot]. In loving memory of **Kate Woodcock** (8 Fairview Lane, Enniskillen), died 29th March 1969, aged 68 yrs. Her husband **Willie** died 17th May 1978, aged 88 yrs.

A3-5 [**CASSIDY** plot]. Pray for **Edward Cassidy** (Derryhowlaght), died 18th January 1968. Also **Mary Ann Quinn** died 17th June 1958. Also their nephew **John Quinn** died 25th March 1970. **Agnes**, wife of **Edward**, died 6th January 1984.

A3-6 [many spaces and mounds].

A3-7 [**McCUTCHEON / PACKENHAM** plot with headstone along with book-shaped pedestal marker]. In loving memory of **Cassie McCutcheon**, died 1st Oct. 1968, aged 54 years. And the **Packenham** Family (Derryaghna). [Pedestal]. In loving memory of **Patrick Packenham**, died 1st Dec. 1969. His wife **Elizabeth** died 18th March 1999.

A3-8 [many spaces and mounds].

A3-9 [base and shaft of a cross; no identification].

A3-10 [space].

[East-West walkway]

A3-11 [space].

A3-12 [shrub].

A3-13 [**McCUSKER** stubby Celtic cross]. **Thomas** 1828-1910. **Brigid** 1835-1915. **Catherine** 1869-1886. **Edward** 1863-1933. **Mary A. Quinn** 1865-1906. Erected by **Ellen McGovern**.

A3-14 [**CONVEY** plot]. In loving memory of a dear wife **Teresa**, died 9th May 1988, aged 56 years. Also grandson **William** died March 1989, aged 11 years.

A3-15 [**McBARRON** plot]. In loving memory of **Bridget**, dear wife and mother, died 15th Feb. 1990, age 57. **Thomas McBarron** died 1950. His wife **Sarah** died 1976. Their son **Hugh** died 1979. **Edward** died 8th Oct. 2011, aged 88 yrs. **John** died 10th Aug. 2020, aged 83 yrs. [Flower holder]. In memory of Mom from **Anne**.

A3-16 [**McBARRON** plot]. In loving memory of **Hugh McBarron**, died 13th Dec. 1961. His wife **Elizabeth** (*nee*

Cassidy) died 5th Nov. 1965. Their son **Hugh Patrick** died 18th April 2006, aged 87 yrs.

A3-17 [spaces and mounds].

ROW A4

A4-1 [**McTEGGART** plot]. In loving memory of **Owenie McTeggart** (Sligo Road), died 21st August 2003, aged 67 years.

A4-2 [spaces to the end of the row].

SECTION B

ROW B1 (starts at the end of the driveway).

B1-1 [Headstone]. Erected by **John Lunney** (Derryhowlaght*) in memory of his father **Bernard Lunney**, his mother **Mary**, his brothers: **Peter, Thomas** and **Andrew**. His sisters: **Mary Ann** and **Margaret**. Also **Bridget**, wife of **Andrew** and **John** his son. Also the above **John Lunney** who died 16th September 1938.

B1-2 [many spaces and mounds].

B1-3 [**McCONNELL** plot]. In loving memory of **Bernard McConnell** (Tully), died 8th Dec. 1928, aged 68 years. His wife **Rose** died 25th Jan. 1950, aged 86 yrs. Their sons: **Thomas** died 15th Aug. 1959, aged 60 yrs. **Patrick** died 15th Dec. 1972, aged 76 yrs. Their daughter **Lizzie** died 6th Oct. 1987, aged 81 yrs.

Transcriptions

B1-4 [spaces].

[North-South sidewalk]

ROW B2

B2-1 [space].

B2-2 [**CULLEN** plot]. In loving memory of **James Cullen**, died 27th April 1980, aged 72 yrs. His wife **Mary Jane** died 28th May 1999, aged 89 yrs. **Aiden Cullen** died 26th December 2013. **Carmel Cullen** died 8th September 2014. Also the **Fee** family.

B2-3 [space].

[East-West sidewalk]

B2-4 [Plot with tall stubby Celtic cross]. Erected by **Peter Murphy** (Skreen*) in loving memory of his father **Patrick Murphy** who died 14th Feb. 1919, aged 84 years. Also his mother **Jane** (*nee* **Cassidy**), who died 14th Feb. 1928, aged 95 years. Also his wife **Alice** (*nee* **Leonard**), who died 11th March 1944, aged 66 years. Also the above **Peter Francis Murphy** who died 14th April 1948, aged 70 years. Also his son **Felix L. Murphy** who died 16th Jan. 1977, aged 69 years. Also his wife **Susan** (**McGovern**) died 30th Jan. 1992, aged 71 years. Also their son **Peter Francis** died 22nd July 2019, aged 60 years.

B2-5 [Plot with broken chain fence]. In memory of **Jane Breslin**, died 31st March 1910. **John** died 30th Jan. 1931. **Margaret** died 14th Aug. 1972.

Transcriptions

B2-6 [spaces and mounds].

ROW B3

B3-1 [space].

B3-2 [**MONTGOMERY** plot with stubby Celtic cross]. In loving memory of **John Montgomery** (Derryinch), died November 1940. His wife **Mary** died April 1941. Their son **James** died 14th Aug. 1988, aged 83 years. And his wife **Mary Ellen** died 30th Nov. 1988, aged 85 years.

B3-3 [Plot]. In loving memory of **Paddy O'Lone**, died 19th May 1977. **William McElhill** died 22nd Jan. 1983. And his wife **Elizabeth (Lizzie)** died 7th April 2014.

[East-West sidewalk]

B3-4 [spaces and mounds].

B3-5 [Plot with Celtic cross tilting backwards]. In loving memory of **Henry Cassidy** who died 5th Jan. 1949.

B3-6 [spaces and mounds].

B3-7 [**McALOON** plot]. In loving memory of **John McAloon**, died 27th Jan. 1956, aged 63. His loving wife **Rose** died 29th Aug. 1963, aged 63. And son **Michael** died 22nd Feb. 1983, aged 52.

Transcriptions

B3-8 [**HOWE** plot]. In loving memory of **Annie Howe** (Tully), died 6th April 1962, aged 54 years. Her husband **Thomas** died 28th July 1965, aged 80 years.

ROW B4

B4-1 [spaces to sidewalk].

[East-West sidewalk]

B4-2 [**BOYLE** plot]. In loving memory of **Marie Boyle** (nee **Owens**), (71 Old Rossorry Road, Enniskillen), died 16th December 2011, aged 63 years.

B4-3 [**GALLAGHER** plot with iron railings and high Celtic cross.] In memory of **John Gallagher** (Arney) who died April 1869. His wife **Jane** died July 1909, aged 90. And their children: **Christy** died 18th October 1918, aged 59. **Jane** died 13th Jan. 1935, aged 83. **Thomas** died 14th Aug. 1935, aged 79. **Felix** died 27th April 1938, aged 77.

B4-4 [**MURPHY** plot]. In loving memory of **Rose Murphy**, died 17th Dec. 1944, aged 80 years. Her husband **John** died 2nd Jan. 1946, aged 93 years. Their daughter **Rose** died 13th May 1982, aged 86 years. Her son **Joe** died 15th July 2011, aged 85 years.

B4-5 [Plot with stubby Celtic cross]. Erected by **Mary A. Maguire** in memory of her beloved brother **John Maguire** (Derryhowlaght) who died 10th Feb. 1919, aged 30 years. Also her father **Peter** who died 30th March 1922, aged 76. **Mary A. McHugh** died March 1935. **Kathleen McHugh** died 15th Aug. 1971. **Renee McHugh** died 8th March 1998. **Philip McHugh** died 17th Feb. 2002.

B4-6 [**McALOON** plot]. In loving memory of **John McAloon** (Skea), died 4th Feb. 1980, aged 56 years. His wife **Mary Ann** died 13th March 2017, aged 95 years. Their baby daughter **Patricia** died 11th Nov. 1957, aged 3 days. Their son **Gary** died 16th Dec. 2020, aged 55 yrs.

ROW B5

B5-1 [space and mounds to sidewalk].

[East-West sidewalk]

B5-2 [**NOLAN** plot]. In loving memory of **Joseph Nolan** (Skea), died 7th July 1974, aged 74 yrs. His wife **Bridget** died 22nd July 1995, aged 78 yrs. His brother **John** died 14th March 1963, aged 64 yrs. His son **Peter** died 5th July 1992, aged 47 yrs. Their daughter **Dympna** died 7th March 2010, aged 68 yrs. Their son **Jody** died 23rd Feb. 2013, aged 70 yrs.

B5-3 [space and mound].

B5-4 [Headstone with lead letters]. Erected by **Richard Herbert** (Enniskillen) in memory of **Thomas Keenan** (Mullylogan), died 30th July 1895, aged 63. And his wife **Mary**, died 19th Feb. 1897, aged 60 years.

Transcriptions

B5-5 [**Keenan** plot with two headstones]. 1. Sacred to the memory of **James Keenan** who depd. this life Sept. 27, 1851, aged 41 years. Also **Bridget Keenan** who depd. this life March 5th 1854, aged 25 years. And their father **Philip Keenan** depd. this life June 14th 1856, aged 90 years. 2. In loving memory of **Hugh** and **Mary Keenan** (Mullanavehy*) and their family.

B5-6 [space].

ROW B6 (empty spaces). [East-West sidewalk has split after Row B5.

ROW B7

B7-1 [**MONAGHAN** plot with recent burial]. Pray for my wife **Bridget Monaghan** (Rossavally*), died 20th Sept. 1964. My parents **Pat** & **Jane Monaghan** died Feb. 1933. My sister **Maggie McManus-Maguire** (Brockagh*) died 18th April 1958. **Patrick**, husband of **Bridget**, died 13th March 1970. Their son **Peter** died 29th June 2005. [Plaque]. **Mary Monaghan** died 30th Dec. 2022.

B7-2 [space to sidewalks].

[East-West sidewalks]

B7-3 [**GALLAGHER** plot]. In loving memory of **Hugh Gallagher** (Derrygiff), died 3 Oct. 1980. His wife **Peggy** died 10 Feb. 1992. His father **Patrick** died 7 Dec. 1942. His mother **Elizabeth** died 1 June 1970. His brother **Willie** died 29 May 1986. **Mary (May)** died 12 May 2013.

B7-4 [many spaces and mounds].

ROW B8

B8-1 [**McBRIEN** plot with stubby Celtic cross and plaque]. In loving memory of **Bridget McBrien** (Rossdoney) who died 30th May 1891. Also her husband **Michael** who died 31st May 1921. **Mary Timony** who died 2nd Feb. 1922. **Francis Gabriel McBrien** died 6th April 1934. **Catherine McBrien** died 14th April 1965. **John McBrien** died 25th Dec. 1975, aged 89 yrs. And his son **John** died 23rd Sept 2012, aged 92 yrs. [Plaque]. In loving memory of **Maura McBrien**, died 20th April 2013, aged 89 years.

B8-2 [spaces to sidewalk].

[East-West sidewalk]

B8-3 [many spaces and mounds].

B8-4 [Roman cross; no identification].

B8-5 [spaces].

Transcriptions

ROW B9

B9-1 [space with small flat stone; no identification].

B9-2 [**MAGUIRE** plot with stubby Celtic cross and plaque]. Sacred heart of Jesus have mercy on the soul of **John Maguire** (Ardtonnagh*) who died 28th April 1953. His wife **Catherine** who died 9th March 1960. Their grandson **James Gerard (Gerry) Maguire** (Mullymesker) 5-8-1949 – 8-1-2021. [Plaque]. In loving memory of **James Gerard Maguire**, late of London, formerly Mullymesker, remembered by his wife **Thelma**, children **Ellen, David** and **Adam**, granddaughter **Rose**.

B9-3 [space between the sidewalks]

B9-4 [spaces and mounds].

B9-5 [Plot]. In loving memory of **Peter McHugh** (Derryhowlaght*) who departed this life 20th Dec. 1924, aged 90 years. Also his wife **Anne** who died 17th Dec. 1930, aged 77 years. Their beloved daughter **Ellen** who died 7th Sept. 1919, aged 20 years. **Peter McHugh** who died 28th April 1969, aged 81 years. His wife **Brigid** who died 21st August 2003, aged 84 years. And all deceased members of the **McHugh** family.

B9-6 [space].

ROW B10 (aligns with end of church).

B10-1 [**McBRIEN** plot]. In loving memory of **James McBrien** (Corraclare), died 27th Dec. 1970. His wife **Jane** died 4th June 1999. And all the deceased members of the family.

B10-2 [**MAGUIRE** plot]. In loving memory of **Hugh Maguire** (Skea), died 10th May 1970, aged 82 yrs. His wife **Ann Jane** died 1st June 1979, aged 81 yrs. Their daughters: **Kathleen** died 1940, aged 10 yrs. **Lily** died 1955, aged 18 yrs. **Peter** died 18th July 1999, aged 64 yrs. **John** died 16th Sept. 2005, aged 77 yrs.

[Sidewalk]

B10-3 [**MURPHY** plot with pink granite headstone]. In loving memory of **James Murphy** (Sessiagh), died 6th April 1958. His wife **Annie** died 29th March 1974. Their son Rev. **Patrick**, S.M., ordained 11th April 1943, died 29th December 2001 (interred in Sidcup, Kent). Their daughter **Patricia** died 9th May 2011. Their son **James** died 31st July 2011.

B10-4 [space to next sidewalk].

B10-5 [spaces and mounds].

B10-6 [**DOLAN** plot]. In loving memory of **John J. Dolan** (Whilliter, Inishmore* [Island]), died 9th Sept. 1978, aged 71 years. His wife **Lelia** died 3rd Dec. 1980, aged 67 years. His sister **Bridget** died 8th Dec. 1979, aged

Transcriptions

75 years. **Patrick Maguire** died 8th Nov. 1993, aged 88 years.

SECTION C
ROW C1

C1-1 [spaces].

C1-2 [Plot with short white decorative Celtic cross]. In loving memory of **McManus** Family and **Cleary** Family.

C1-3 [spaces and mounds].

C1-4 [**LUNNY** plot]. In loving memory of **Mary Ellen Lunny** (Inishmore* [Island]), died 9 May 1975, aged 65. Her husband **James** died 27 March 1979, aged 79. Their daughter-in-law **Kathleen** (*nee* **Scallon**) died 23 November 2010, aged 66.

C1-5 [spaces and mounds].

C1-6 [**OWENS** plot]. **Andrew Owens** (Sessiagh) died 14th Feb. 1956. His wife **Ellen** died 4th Feb. 1973. Their son **Philip** died 30th June 2001. And his wife **Mary T.** died 23rd June 2010, aged 92 years.

C1-7 [**OWENS** plot]. In loving memory of **Andrew Owens** (Sessiagh) who died 23rd February 2001, aged 82 years. Also his wife **Anna** who died 23rd February 2003, aged 80 years. **Francis Owens** (Sessiagh) died 4th August 1958, aged 80 years.

Transcriptions

C1-8 [BARTLEY plot]. In loving memory of **James Bartley** (Skea), died 21st April 1961, aged 64 years. His wife **Margaret Ellen** died 23rd June 1974, aged 75 years. His grandson **Myles Patrick** died 5th June 2017, aged 45 years. His son **Myles** died 25th Feb. 2018, aged 84 years.

C1-9 [many spaces and mounds].

C1-10 [Headstone dangerously tilted backward, covered in ivy]. Erected by **Michael Kerrin** of Drumbrughas in memory of his father **Manus Kerrin** who departed this life January 10th 1858, aged 81 years.

ROW C2

C2-1 [Headstone with lead letters, tilting backward]. Erected by **Philip McGivney** in memory of his mother **Mary**, died 5th Nov. 1849, aged 37 years. Also his father **Owen** died 3rd Feb. 1892, aged 87 years.

C2-2 [Headstone]. Erected by **William Greene** in loving memory of his mother **Catherine Greene**, died 27th February 1874, aged 60 years. Also his father **Patrick Greene** who died 24th July 1877, aged 75 years.

C2-3 [spaces and mounds].

C2-4 [shrub].

C2-5 [**CARSON** headstone]. In loving memory of **William Carson**, died 11th May 1959. **Bridget Carson** died 21st Jan. 1975. **Jane Boyle** died 3rd June 1981. **James Boyle** died 4th Aug. 1982.

C2-6 [spaces].

C2-7 [**TIMONEY** plot with two headstones]. 1. The **Timoney** Family (Druminiskill, Machen). 2. [Repaired crack running through numbers; age uncertain.] Erected by **Josephine Timoney** in memory of her dearly beloved husband **John Timoney**, Colour Sergeant 27th Enniskillings, who departed this life 20th January 1880, aged 35 [?] years.

C2-8 [spaces and mounds with a flat stone in front of C3-7].

C2-9 [Headstone with lead letters]. Erected by **Hannah O'Brien** of New York in memory of my beloved parents **Noher Boyle** of Rossavally* and his wife **Hannah**.

C2-10 [spaces and mounds to the end of row].

ROW C3

C3-1 [space].

C3-2 [**MONTGOMERY** plot with stubby Celtic cross]. In loving memory of **Annie Montgomery** (Tonyteige*), died 28 Feb. 1953. Her daughter **Margaret** died 26 July 1978. Her husband **Patrick** died 13 April 1993. And son **John Patrick** died 18 March 1945 in infancy.

C3-3 [Plot with two headstones]. 1. Erected by the Republicans of Fermanagh in proud memory of Vol[unteer] **Phillip Cassidy** who took up arms to establish an Irish Republic, Post Office, Dublin, 1916. 2. In loving memory of **James Cassidy** (Aghanagh), died 6th July 1923, aged 84 years. His father **Patrick Cassidy** died 7th Sept. 1855, aged 50 years. And his mother **Anne Cassidy** died 12th Jan. 1895, aged 97 years. Also his wife **Mary** died 23rd March 1934. And his sons: **Patrick** died 7th June 1933. **James Philip** died 5th May 1938. **Thomas Gregory Cassidy** died 2nd Aug. 1957.

C3-4 [**CORRIGAN** plot with fresh grave]. **Hugh Corrigan** (Rossdoney), died 3rd June 1973, aged 84 yrs. His wife **Kate** died 8th Feb. 1986, aged 84 yrs. Their son **Richard** died 7th Feb. 2005, aged 66 yrs. [Plaque]. **Mena Corrigan** died 1st March 2023.

C3-5 [Plot with stubby Celtic cross]. In loving memory of **Anna Christina Corrigan** (Rossdoney) who died 28th December 1949, aged 14 years. And of her brother **Liam** who died 19th November 1932, aged 5 weeks. And of her father **Patrick Corrigan** who died 19th April 1957, aged 60 years. And of her mother **Margaret** (*nee* **Donohoe**) who died 22nd November 2002, aged 97 years. And members of the **Corrigan** Family interred in this grave.

C3-6 [space with a possible sunken headstone].

C3-7 [**TIMONEY** plot with headstone and flat marker; note spelling variation]. In loving memory of **John Timoney** (Rossdoney), died 19th Feb. 1951. His wife **Cassie Jane** died 22nd May 1953. And their son **John Patrick** died 14th April 1978. And their son **Jimmy** died 4th August 1997. [Flat]. Erected by **James Timeney** of Rossdoney in memory of his son **Patrick** who departed this life 6th September 1864, aged 56 years. Also his beloved wife **Margaret Timeney** who departed this life 7th April 1875, aged 74 years.

C3-8 [**McMANUS** plot with stubby Celtic cross]. Sacred heart of Jesus have mercy on the soul of **James McManus** (Drumane) who died 25th April 1938. His father **John McManus** who died 7th February 1937. His mother **Brigid McManus** who died 20th February 1944. His wife **Kathleen** who died 14th May 1994.

C3-9 [Plot with Celtic cross]. **Patrick McManus** died 8th May 1951. His wife **Margaret McManus** died 1st Nov. 1938. Their granddaughter **Margaret Mary McManus** died 11th March 1941. And their son **Conor McManus** died 4th Aug. 1951.

C3-10 [space and mounds].

C3-11 [**FLYNN/O'PREY** plot]. In loving memory of **John P. Flynn**, died 19th Jan. 1933. His father **James** died 7th Oct. 1939. His mother **Mary** died 14th Aug. 1945. His brother **Jimmy** died 7th Sept. 1967. Also **John O'Prey** died 17th June 1991. His wife **Mary Jane** died 19th April 2003.

C3-12 [spaces].

[East -West sidewalk]

C3-13 [spaces and mounds].

ROW C4

C4-1 [Narrow plot]. In loving memory of **Catherine Maxwell**, died 11th Dec. 1905, aged 74 yrs. **Kathleen Maxwell** died 30th Dec. 2007, aged 93 yrs.

C4-2 [space and mounds].

C4-3 [Plot with stubby Celtic cross]. In loving memory of **James Cox** (Derrychurra) who died 19th August 1951, aged 68 years. His grandson **Vincent Cox** who died 2nd November 1956, aged 4 years. His wife **Ellen Cox** who died 9th Dec. 1973, aged 92 years. His son **John** died 20th Nov. 1984, aged 71 years. (**John**'s wife) **Frances** died 4th Sept. 2009, aged 90 years.

C4-4 [space].

C4-5 [Headstone; badly shaled]. Erected by **Michael Macken** (Rossdoney) in memory of his son **Owen Macken** who died 6th July 1874, aged 18 years. Also his beloved wife **Bridget Macken** who died 12th August 1875, aged 63 years.

Transcriptions

C4-6 [spaces and mounds].

C4-7 [Short gray decorative Celtic cross]. Pray for the souls of the **Lunney** family (Gortdonaghy, Bellanaleck*).

C4-8 [Headstone]. In loving memory of **James Curran** (Skea), died 12th March 1906. Also his wife **Sarah Curran** died 31st March 1912. Also their son **John** died 26th Sept. 1914. And their daughter **Mary Jane** died 21st Dec. 1914. Erected by **William** and **Peter Curran**.

C4-9 [spaces and mounds].

C4-10 [Headstone; years of death for **Bernard** and **Hugh** are suspect. **Bernard** was in the 1911 census]. Sacred to the memory of **Rodger Mackell**, died Feb. 1847. Also his wife **Ellen** died Oct. 1865. Their son **Bernard** died March 1910. Their son **Hugh** died June 1915. Erected by their daughter **Susan**. Also of **Susan Mackell** who died 28th Nov. 1924, aged 72 yrs.

C4-11 [spaces].

C4-12 [Narrow **BRODISON** plot; no other details].

C4-13 [spaces and mounds].

C4-14 [Plot with Celtic cross]. Erected by **Pat McGurrin** (Crockareddy) in memory of his parents and brothers.

C4-15 [Headstone]. Erected by **Patrick O'Neil** of Derreens in memory of his beloved daughter **Catherine** who departed this life April 23rd 1852.

Transcriptions

C4-16 [rock; possible grave marker].

C4-17 [spaces to sidewalk].

East-West sidewalk.

C4-18 [spaces and mounds].

C4-19 [Plot with short gray decortive Celtic cross]. Pray for the **Boyle** Family of Rossdoney and Tonyteige*.

C4-20 [Plot with small Celtic cross and plaque]. Pray for the **Boyle** Family of Rossdoney and Tonyteige*. [Plaque]. Precious memories of **Lorraine**, died 10 Sept. 1986, aged 2 yrs. 9 mths.

ROW C5 (short row merging with C6).

C5-1 [spaces].

C5-2 [**DRUMM** plot with two headstones]. 1. In loving memory of **Philip Drumm** (Sessiagh), died 8th Nov. 1942. And his wife **Catherine Jane** died 21st Sept. 1952. And their son **John Thomas** died 10th April 1995. And their daughter **Kathleen** died 7th Dec. 1999. 2. Erected by **Mary McCurrin** in memory of her beloved husband **Michael McCurrin** who departed this life May the 20th 1855, aged 62 years.

ROW C6

C6-1 [space and mound].

C6-2 [rock; possible burial marker].

C6-3 [space and mounds].

C6-4 [**OWENS** plot with two headstones]. 1. In loving memory of **Hugh Patrick Owens** (Sessiagh), died 24th June 1986, aged 78 yrs. His father **Tom** died 13th Sept. 1944. His mother **Annie** died 15th July 1939. His brother **Francis Thomas** died 15th Dec. 1942. His grandson baby **Damian** died 9th Aug. 1980. His wife **Rose Ann (Cissie)** died 31st May 1998, aged 80 yrs. 2. Erected by **Philip McGivney** (Rossdoney) in memory of his beloved mother **Mary** who departed this life 24th 1856, aged 28 years. Also his father **Michael McGivery** who departed this life 24th April 1858, aged 34 years.

C6-5 [**OWENS** plot with two headstones]. 1. [Stubby Celtic cross]. **Philip Owens** (The Ford), died 24/11/1965, aged 90 years. His wife **Anne** died 11/11/1927, aged 42 years. And their children: **Margaret**, **Mary** and **Helen Cecilia**. And their son **Philip** died 21/10/2000, aged 82 years. 2. Erected by **John Owens** of Sessiagh* in memory of his father **Maurice Owens**, who departed this life 24th February 1953, aged 80 years. Also his mother **Bridget** who departed this life 3rd March 1852, aged 84 years. Also his

Transcriptions

son **Nathaniel Owens** who departed this life 30th January 1868, aged 24 years.

C6-6 [space with mound with small cross; possibly child's burial].

C6-7 [many spaces and mounds].

C6-8 [shaft of a cross; no identification].

C6-9 [Large **MAGUIRE** plot with headstone and plaque]. In loving memory of **John Patrick Maguire** (Mullymesker, formerly Ardtonnagh*), born 17-3-1919. Died 4-12-1991. His dearly beloved wife **Ellen Nora** (*nee* **Magee**), born 20-3-1922. Died 10-4-2012. [Plaque on pedestal]. Pray for **James Quigley** (Mullymesker) who died 8th December 1938. And his wife **Bridget** who died 1932. Her sister Mrs. **Margaret Rooney** who died 9th June 1943.

C6-10 [spaces and mounds to sidewalk; row ends].

ROW C7

C7-1 [**FARLEY** plot]. In loving memory of **John Farley** (Derreens* East), died 3rd Jan. 1958, aged 77. His wife **Elizabeth** died 1st Jan. 1966, aged 85. Their son **Eugene** died 5th April 1990. Their son **Patrick Joseph** died 23rd May 1993. And their daughters: **Susan Dolan** died 11th Aug. 1977 (Enniskillen). **Mary Dray** died 7th Dec. 1984

(Maidstone [ENG]). **Margaret McKinney** died 15th Sept. 2011 (Derry).

C7-2 [space].

C7-3 [Plot with short white Celtic cross; three plaques]. 1. **James Gilheaney** (Skea, Arney, Enniskillen), who died April 9th 1964, aged 50 years. 2. In loving memory of **Mary (Molly) Gilheaney**, died 23rd April 1980. 3. In loving memory of the **McTeggart** family.

C7-4 [spaces and mounds].

C7-5 [**BRADY** plot]. In loving memory of **Winnie Brady**, died 23rd February 2014, aged 78 years. **Francis J. McTeggart**, cousin, died 15th July 1950, aged 11 years.

C7-6 [**McGAHEY** plot]. **Thomas J. McGahey** (Derryagna) died 20 August 1963. His wife **Kathleen** died 9 July 1979. Their baby son **Thomas J.** Their son **John** died 13 August 2016.

C7-7 [**McTEGGART** plot]. In loving memory of **Owen McTeggart** (33 Old Henry Street, Enniskillen), died 4th June 1971. Also his wife **Sarah McTeggart** died 10th Jan. 1992. **Martina Kelly** died 23rd June 2018. [Plaque gave her age as 46].

C7-8 [many spaces and mounds running parallel to North-South sidewalk].

C7-9.[Plot with iron railings and stubby Celtic cross]. Sacred heart of Jesus have mercy on the soul of **Patrick**

Sheridan (Lisbofin), who died 12th March 1951, aged 81 years. Also his wife **Susan** who died 18th Jan. 1975, aged 91 years.

C7-10 [space before sidewalk turns East-West].

[East-West sidewalk]

C7-11 [spaces and mounds].

C7-12 [**QUIGLEY** plot with stubby Celtic cross]. Sacred heart of Jesus have mercy on the souls of our beloved parents: **Francis Quigley** who died Nov. 1st 1928. And **Mary Anne Quigley** who died Sept. 19th 1957. Their son **Eugene Quigley** died 17th Oct. 1973. His wife **Josephine** died 9th May 1986. Their son **Noel** died 16th June 1973.

C7-13 [**JUDGE** plot]. In loving memory of **John Judge** (Cloonatrig*), died 16th June 1971, aged 64 years. His wife **Mary** died 5th Feb. 2006, aged 90 yrs. Granddaughters: **Ann Elizabeth** died 10th Jan. 1975, aged 4 ½ yrs. **Jennifer Marie** died 4th Oct. 1986, aged 14 yrs.

C7-14 [Plot with decorative iron railings and high Celtic cross; inscriptions on two sides of base]. Erected to the memory of **Patrick Doogan** of Rossavally,* who died 14th January 1853, aged 56 years. Also **Catherine Doogan**, wife of the above, who died 17th Dec. 1883, aged 76 years. Also **Charles Patrick Doogan**, son of the above, M.P. for East Tyrone 1895 till 1906, who died at Inishmore 15th

June 1906, aged 69 years. [Left side of base]. **John Doogan** died Dec. 24, 1917, aged 84 years. His wife **Ellen** died Jan. 16, 1914, aged 62 yrs.

ROW C8

C8-1 [Headstone oriented backwards to grave; inscription left out father's name]. Erected to the memory of father who died May 20th 1854, aged 85 years. And to my brother **Hugh** who died March 1865, aged 65 years. By **Michael Magevney**, Memphis, Tennessee.

C8-2 [spaces and mounds].

C8-3 [**REIHILL** plot]. In loving memory of **Anne Reilhill**, died 20th Oct. 1958. Her husband **Patrick** died 15th Feb. 1976. And their son **Joseph** died 17th Dec. 1977. Their son-in-law **Thomas Lunny** died 12th Aug. 2000. His wife **Mary** died 21st June 2013.

[East-West sidewalk]

C8-4 [spaces and mounds].

C8-5 [Smashed sarcophagus; some ages uncertain]. Erected by **Neal Macken** of Derryhowlaght in memory of his beloved sons, *i.e.* **Patrick** who departed this life Oct. 15th 1837, aged 7 years. **Robert** who departed this life March 1847, aged 47 years. **William** who departed this life Sept. 23rd 1852, aged 12 [?] years. **Francis** who departed this life June 10th 1858, aged 21 years.

C8-6A [**McMANUS** plot]. In loving memory of **Paul McManus** (Sessiagh), died 17th Feb. 1973, aged 16 mths. His sister **Carmel** died 31st August 1986, aged 8 mths. Their parents: **Hugh** died 10th December 2020, aged 74. **Patsy** died 20th July 2021, aged 75.

C8-6B [Headstone at edge of plot; relationship unclear]. Erected by **Owen Lilly** of Sessiagh* and his three brothers **Patt, Matthew** and **Denis** in memory of their father **John Lilly** who departed this life July 28, 1838, aged 67.

C8-7 [Plot with small Celtic cross]. In memory of **Jane Corrigan** (Sessiagh).

C8-8 [**KEENAN** plot with two headstones]. 1. In loving memory of **Benny Keenan** (Bellanaleck). His wife **Betty**. His parents **Patrick & Mary**. Also his brothers **Peter & Patrick**. **Phil** and his wife **Ann**. 2. Erected by **Bernard Keenan** of Rossavally* in memory of his beloved wife **Mary Keenan** who departed this life July 8th 1863, aged 53 [?] years. Also **Ann Keenan** who departed this life March 31st 1863, aged 14 years.

C3-9 [spaces and mounds].

ROW C9

C9-1 [spaces and mounds].

C9-2 [High Celtic cross]. Erected by **Ellen Creegan** in loving memory of her dear husband **Francis Creegan**

(John's Row, Westport, Co. Mayo), who died on the 2nd June 1921, aged 44 years.

C9-3 [spaces and mounds].

C9-4 [Headstone tilting dangerously forward]. Erected by **Philip McManus** in memory of his father **John McManus** (Drumbrughas*)) who died 6th May 1869, aged 58 years. Also his mother **Elizabeth McManus** who died 3rd June 1874, aged 61 years. And also his brother **Joseph** who died April 3rd 1861, aged 2 years and 8 months.

C9-5 [space].

C9-6 [rock; may be a burial marker].

C9-7 [spaces and mounds].

C9-8 [Small Roman cross; no identification].

C9-9 [many spaces and mounds].

C9-10 [Small Celtic cross]. **Hugh Nolan** died 14th Nov. 1981.

C9-11 [many spaces and mounds].

C9-12 [**MURPHY** plot]. In loving memory of **James Murphy** (Derryinch), who died 11th April 1964, aged 78 years. Also wife **Mary Anne** who died 25th April 1965, aged 75 years.

C9-13 [Plot with pipe railings]. In loving memory of **John McGovern** (Rossavally*), who died 10th December 1942. His wife **Elizabeth** who died 2nd January 1954. Their sons:

Transcriptions

James who died 14th January 1956. Michael who died 29th March 1964.

C9-14 [Small headstone hidden under tree]. Erected [for] **Pat Maguire** (Skea), August 1884.

ROW C10

C10-1 [Massive **CORRIGAN** plot with lead letters missing from base inscription]. Erected by **Thomas Corrigan** (Tully) in memory of his parents: **Nathaniel** died Oct. 10 1845, aged 56. **Bridget** 5th Jan. 1899, aged 84. His sister **Mary Slavin** died Oct.6, 1887, aged 50. His brother **Bernard** 29th Oct. 1889, aged 60. And his wife **Anne** died May 30, 1886, 41 yrs. Also **Nathaniel Corrigan** (Tully) died 25th Jan. 1955, aged 62 yrs. And **Sarah Corrigan** (Cloonatrig*) died 3rd Jan. 1947, aged 60 yrs. Also **Nathaniel Corrigan** died 5th March 1953, aged 71 yrs. [Left panel]. In loving memory of **Minnie Corrigan** (Tully), died 3rd Sept. 1986, aged 86 yrs. Her beloved son **Patrick (Packie) Corrigan** died 1st April 2006, aged 69 yrs. [Right panel]. In loving memory of **Nathaniel Corrigan**, died 6th July 1995, aged 77 yrs. His wife **Teresa** died 3rd Feb. 2002, aged 73 yrs. Their son **Donal** died 20th April 2000, aged 37 yrs.

C10-2 [small space].

C10-3 [**CORRIGAN** plot]. In loving memory of **Patrick Corrigan** (Mulrod, Tamlaght), died 15th Nov. 1981, aged 71 years. Also his beloved wife **Philomena** died 7th Feb. 1992, aged 63 years.

C10-4 [Stubby Celtic cross headstone]. Sacred heart of Jesus have mercy on the soul of **Andrew Lynch** (Killywillin*), who died 20th September 1939. And his wife **Margaret** who died 14th March 1953.

C10-5 [spaces and mounds].

C10-6 [**GILLEECE** plot]. Pray for the souls of **John** and **Anne Gilleece** (Sessiagh). Also **Hugh Gilleece** and all the deceased members of the family. Their son **John** died 9th Feb. 1990.

C10-7 [**HEALY** plot]. In loving memory of **Thomas D'Arcy**, died March 1912. His wife **Bridget** (*nee* **Fox**) died March 1927. **James Healy** died 23rd Aug. 1960. His wife **Catherine** (*nee* **D'Arcy**) died Aug. 27th 1954. **James Robinson** died 31st Oct. 1975. His wife **Bridget** (*nee* **Healy**) died 30th Nov. 1974.

C10-8 [space].

C10-9 [**GILROY** plot]. In loving memory of **Denis Gilroy**, died 25th May 1942. His wife **Mary Alice** died 3rd Oct. 1953. Also their six children. Also **Denis Gilroy** died 25th Jan. 1975. And **Kathleen Gilroy** died 27th Aug. 1977. **Brigid Gilroy** died 1st Aug. 1984.

Transcriptions

C10-10 [spaces].

C10-11 [Headstone]. Erected in memory of **Ann Maguire**, died 22nd April 1888, aged 40 years. **Michael Maguire** died 14th April 1886, aged 17 years. **James Maguire** died 9th July 1909, aged 74 years. **Ann Maguire** died 15th July 1918, aged 80 years. Erected by **James Maguire**.

C10-12 [**McELGUNN** plot with stubby Celtic cross]. Sacred heart of Jesus have mercy on the soul of **Thomas McElgunn** (Crockareddy), who died 3rd Nov. 1957. His sister **Mary** who died 21st August 1954. His brother **John** who died 15th Oct. 1944. Their nephew **Thomas Alex Maguire** who died 3rd April 2005.

C10-13 [spaces and mounds].

C10-14 [**CASSIDY** plot with high Celtic cross]. **Patrick Cassidy** (Sessiagh) died 26th June 1902. His wife **Catherine Cassidy** died 9th Sept. 1912. And **Mary Josephine Cassidy**, wife of **Bernard Cassidy**, died 16th June 1956. Also **Bernard Cassidy** died 6th August 1970. Also **Tessie Cassidy** died 4th August 2002. And her husband **Charlie** died 24th April 2008.

C10-15 [High Celtic cross with inscriptions on front and back of base]. Erected by **Elizabeth M. Riley** (Boston, USA), in memory of her grandfather and grandmother **Daniel McManus** and **Ann Dolan McManus**, her father and mother **Patrick McAloon** and **Ann**

McManus McAloon, for uncle **Andrew McAloon**, and her brother **William John McAloon**. [Back]. Pray for the souls of **Joseph Maguire, Jane Maguire, Patrick Maguire, Ann Jane Maguire**, died 16th May 1977.

C10-16 [spaces and mounds].

C10-17 [Plot with decorative iron railings and stubby Celtic cross]. **Matthew Snow** (Sessiagh) died 31st May 1966, aged 60 years. His wife **Mary** died 21st October 1977, aged 75 years.

C10-18 [small space].

C10-19 [**DOOGAN** plot with stubby Celtic cross]. (Derryhowlaght). To the glory of God and in loving memory of **Patrick Doogan**, died 1st March 1915. **Ann Doogan** died 8th Dec. 1926. Also their daughters: **Alice** died 15th Sept. 1907. **Margaret Jane Doogan** died 29th June 1919.

C10-20 [**CORRIGAN** plot]. In loving memory of **John Corrigan** (Derryinch), died 31st Oct. 1941. His wife **Bridget** died 17th Nov. 1952. Their daughter-in-law **Annie** died 24th Dec. 1978. Their son **John** died 16th Oct. 1996, aged 85 years. His son **John (Sean)** died 4th Aug. 2004, aged 49 years.

C10-21 [spaces and mounds].

Transcriptions

C10-22 [**LUNNEY** headstone hidden under large tree]. (Rosscairn). In fond memory of **Terence James**, died 20th July 1983. **John Francis** died 28th April 1984. **Kathleen Foy** died 19th July 2002. Above were family of the late **John & Bridget Lunney** (Rosscairn, High Bridge), also interred here.

SECTION D [Burials of past priests].

D-1 [Plot]. Pray for the Very Rev. Canon **Kevin Slowey**, parish priest of Cleenish 1970-1988, who died 8th July 1994.

D-2 [Plot]. Pray for the soul of Rev. **John McManus**, C.C., died 1st January 1976.

D-3 [Plot with high Celtic cross]. Pray for the soul of Very Rev. **Michael McElroy**, parish priest of Cleenish who died 16th November 1964, aged 69 years.

D-4 [Plot with high Celtic cross]. Of your charity pray for the repose of the soul of Rev. **Patrick J. McManus**, C.C., Inishkeen*, who died on the 2nd February 1952, in the thirty-first year of his priesthood.

D-5 [Plot with high Celtic cross]. Pray for the repose of the soul of the Very Rev. **Eugene** Canon **MacMahon**, P.P., Chancellor of Clogher, who was born 21st June 1853, ordained priest June 1880, appointed parish priest of

Cleenish 1900, and died 8th December 1942. Erected by his parishioners.

D-6 [Plot with high Celtic cross]. Pray for the repose of the soul of the Very Rev. **John Donnelly**, P.P., who was born 7th July 1887, ordained priest 19th April 1914, C.C. Arney 1914-1915, C.C. Belcoo 1922-1925, ADM. Cleenish 1939-1945, appointed parish priest of Cleenish 17th February 1943, and died 13th February 1955.

SECTION E

ROW E1 (empty row).

ROW E2

E2-1 [Two temporary wooden cross]. **Edward Buchholz** died 8th November 2021. **Agnes Buchholz** died 3rd June 2022.

E2-2 [Temporary wooden cross]. **Brendan Boyle** died 23rd Dec. 2022.

E2-3 [space].

[Sidewalk between rows]

Transcriptions

ROW E3

E3-1 [O'CONNOR plot]. In loving memory of **Mary Patricia (Pat)**, devoted mother, grandmother and great-grandmother, died 19th Jan. 2020, aged 80 years.

E3-2 [OWENS plot]. Cherished memories of **Francis Owens**, died 3rd November 2020, aged 66 years.

E3-3 [Temporary wooden cross]. In loving memory of **Pete McKay**, died 7th August 2021, aged 74 years.

E3-4 [MAGUIRE plot]. In loving memory of **Gabriel Maguire**, a beloved husband, father and grandfather, died 20th September 2021, aged 76 years.

E3-5 [space].

ROW E4

E4-1 [McCUTCHEON plot]. Cherished memories of **Rosealeen**, 21st Oct. 1934 – 1st April 2016.

E4-2 [McALOON plot]. In memory of **Jim**, a dear husband, father, grandfather and great-grandfather, died 2nd March 2017, aged 89 years.

E4-3 [Plot]. In loving memory of **Andy Cullen**, died 31st July 2017, aged 68 years.

E4-4 [COLE plot]. In loving memory of **Jonathan (Johnny)**, died 9th August 2018, aged 89 years.

Transcriptions

E4-5 [KINAHAN plot]. In loving memory of **John Hilary Kinahan**, beloved husband, father, and grandfather, 16th July 1928 – 27th June 2019.

E4-6 [McALOON plot]. Treasured memories of **Mary McAloon** (nee **Murtagh**), 28-7-1950 – 20-8-2019. Jesus I trust in you.

[Sidewalk between rows]

ROW E5

E5-1 [Plot]. In loving memory of **Laura Spence** (3, The Meadows), died 2nd March 2012.

E5-2 [BANNON plot]. In loving memory of a beloved husband, father and grandfather **Terence Bannon** (Sessiagh), died 26th April 2013, aged 59 years.

E5-3 [BARTLEY plot]. In loving memory of **James Oliver (Jim) Bartley**, 30th June 1936 – 29th November 2011.

E5-4 [MAGUIRE plot]. In loving memory of **Vincent Maguire** (Brockagh), born 4th August 1930, died 2nd July 2014.

E5-5 [MORRIS plot]. In loving memory of a devoted husband and father **Daniel (Dan) Morris**, died 26th December 2014, aged 37 years.

Transcriptions

E5-6 [McAULEY plot]. In loving memory of **Sheila McAuley**, 25-10-1933 – 08-04-2015. Her husband **James** 28-11-1925 – 29-10-2019.

E5-7 [Temporary wooden cross]. **Mary Gilbride** died 30th August 2015.

E5-8 [OWENS plot]. In loving memory of **Rosealeen Owens** (Sessiagh), died 31st August 2015, devoted wife, mother and grandmother, aged 67 years. And her loving husband **T.P.** died 9th July 2019, aged 76 years.

[Sidewalk between rows]

ROW E6

E6-1 [HOWE plot]. In loving memory of **Mary Ellen (Cissie) Howe**, died 13th April 2004, aged 74 years.

E6-2 [COX plot]. In loving memory of a dear husband and father **Patrick (Pady) Cox** (Tulleevin Park, Enniskillen), died 18th March 2005, aged 56 years.

E6-3 [THOMPSON plot]. In loving memory of a dear wife and mother **Eithne Mary**, died 20th April 2005, aged 34 years.

E6-4 [CORRIGAN plot]. In loving memory of Sister **Mary Jacinta Corrigan** (Mary Catherine, Convent of Mercy, Castleblaney and Rossdoney), died 14th July 2007, aged 71 years.

E6-5 [Plot]. **Sean Farmer** (Drumawill, Enniskillen). Precious memories of a deeply loved husband, father and grandfather, passed away 14th September 2008, aged 67 years.

E6-6 [**McBRIEN** plot]. In loving memory of **Eileen McBrien** (*nee* **McGovern**), (Derrygiff), 8th Feb. 1955 – 6th March 2009.

E6-7 [**McTEGGART** plot with a recent burial]. In loving memory of **Elizabeth (Betty) McTeggart**, died 24th April 2009. [Plaque]. In loving memory of **Patrick (Paddy) McTeggart**, 24th February. 1938, 30th January 2023.

E6-8 [**BOYLE** plot]. In loving memory of **Michael**, died 20th June 2009, aged 54 years.

[Sidewalk with railing between rows]

ROW E7

E7-1 [**COYLE** plot]. In loving memory of a loving husband and father **Gabriel** died 27th March 1998, aged 54.

E7-2 [Plot]. Baby **Anna Maureen Keenan** 27th October 1999.

E7-3 [**MARTIN** plot]. Treasured memories of a beautiful daughter and sister **Leanne Jennifer**, died 6th December 1999, aged 4 years 9 months.

E7-4 [**McKENZIE** plot]. In loving memory of **Desmond McKenzie** (Skea, Culky P.O.), died 29th December 1999, aged 70 years. And his wife **Yvonne** died 1st April 2011, aged 77 years. Remembered by your loving son **Gerard**.

E7-5 [**HENSHALL** plot]. Baby **Matthew Henshall**, 30th Sept. 2002.

E7-6 [**BOYLE** plot]. In loving memory of **Declan**, a loving son and brother, died 4th August 2003, aged 23 years.

ROW E8

E8-1 [**OWENS** plot]. In loving memory of **James Owens**, died 26th June 1996, aged 82 years. And his loving wife **Bridget** died 17th January 2002, aged 90 years.

E8-2 [**MURPHY** plot]. In loving memory of **Irene Murphy** (Carneyhill, Bellanaleck), died 24th Sept. 1996, aged 44 years.

E8-3 [**WARD** plot]. In loving memory of **Patrick Ward** (Inishmore*), died 7th Dec. 1996, aged 70 years. His wife **Agnes** died 24th March 2008, aged 81 years.

E8-4 [**O'BRIEN** plot]. In loving memory of **Ann O'Brien** (*nee* **McGurn**) (Arney), died 30th March 1998, aged 59 years.

E8-5 [**QUINN** plot]. In loving memory of **Theresa Quinn** (*nee* **McGurn**), beloved wife and mother, born 29th December 1945, died 21st June 1999. Her husband **John Patrick**, born 22nd February 1945, died 27th October 2010.

E8-6 [**McHUGH** plot]. In loving memory of **Bernard**, died 7th February 2002, aged 72 years. His wife **Alice** died 19th September 2012, aged 91 years.

E8-7 [**OWENS** plot]. Pray for the soul of **John F. (Sean)**, who died 21st June 2003, aged 86 years. And his wife **Rita** who died 24th July 2018, aged 95 years. Also their beloved son **Malachy** who died in Sydney, Australia 8th September 2020, aged 66 years.

[Sidewalk between rows]

ROW E9

E9-1 [**McGURN** plot]. In loving memory of **James McGurn**, died 17th August 1991, aged 82 years. And his wife **Margaret** died 18th January 1999, aged 89 years. Their daughter **Sheila** died 27th April 2003, aged 54 years. Their son **Eamon** died 19th August 2017, aged 80 years. **Gerry** died 16th February 2021, aged 76 years.

E9-2 [**MURPHY** plot]. In loving memory of **Charles Murphy** (Drumgallan* and formerly of Skreen*), 14th April 1920 – 6th July 1992. His wife **Teres**a (nee **McAuley**) 16th January 1927 – 6th April 2017.

E9-3 [**SHEERIN** plot]. In loving memory of **Catherine Sheerin** (Derryhowlaght), died 2nd February 1994, aged 82 years.

E9-4 [**FARMER** plot]. In loving memory of **Jim Farmer**, died 27th April 1994. His wife **Bridget** died 17th August 1995.

E9-5 [**GILHEANEY** plot]. In loving memory of **John Gilheaney**, died 18th Jan. 1995, aged 80 yrs. His brother **Hugh** died 15th April 2016, aged 91 yrs.

E9-6 [**CONNORS** plot]. In loving memory of **Patricia Connors** (Bellanaleck), died 14th October 1996, aged 54 years. And her husband **Philip (Phil)** 25th August 2010, aged 80 years.

[Sidewalk between rows]

ROW E10

E10-1 [**CORNYN** plot]. In loving memory of **Bridget Cornyn**, died 7th June 1988, aged 68 years. Her husband **Murty** died 28th May 2012, aged 89 years. Their son **Murty** died 8th June 2018, aged 63 years.

E10-2 [**O'BRIEN** plot]. In loving memory of **Jim O'Brien** (Oakfield), died 24th January 1989, aged 80 years. His wife **Annie** (*nee* **Gilleece**) died 30th January 1999, aged 80 years.

E10-3 [**QUIGLEY** plot with stubby Celtic cross]. In loving memory of **William John Quigley** (Mullanavehy*), died

17 May 1989, aged 76 yrs. His brother **Eddie** died 10 August 2001, aged 85 yrs. **William John**'s wife **Bridget** died 27 April 2018, aged 91 yrs.

E10-4 **[McTEGGART** plot]. In loving memory of **Frances Ann McTeggart** (Corraglass*), died 28th Oct. 1989.

E10-5 [space].

[Sidewalk between rows]

ROW E11

E11-1 [Plot]. Baby **Margaret McAdam**, 27th March 1982.

E11-2 [space].

E11-3 **[MEEHAN** plot]. In loving memory of baby **Patrick Meehan**, died 1st August 1983. His brother **Mark Eugene** died 25th May 1999, aged 17 yrs. Their niece **Lisa** died 6th July 2014, aged 23 yrs. Their mother **Mary Teresa** died 12th April 2016, aged 72 years.

E11-4 [Plot]. In loving memory of **John Drumm** (Mullanavehy*), died 16th Nov. 1983, aged 74 years. His wife **Mary** died 14th 1997, aged 77 years.

E11-5 [**GILHEANEY** plot]. In loving memory of **Jim Gilheaney**, died 5th June 1984, aged 43 years.

E11-6 [**QUIGLEY** plot with headstone and plaque]. In loving memory of **Winifred Quigley** (Bellanaleck), died 27 Aug. 1987, aged 68 yrs. Her husband **Patrick** died 21st May 1988, aged 77 yrs. Their daughter **Bernadette Large** died 6th Dec. 2010, aged 50 yrs. [Plaque]. In loving memory of **Bernard (Bertie) Quigley**, died 27th August 1995, aged 45 years. Interred in Portaferry.

ROW E12

E12-1 [**McBRIEN** plot]. In loving memory of **Mary McBrien** (Rossdoney), died 1st November 1979, aged 69 years. Her husband **Patrick** died 18th May 1980, aged 75 years. Also their infant son **John Francis** died 21st April 1939. Son **Brenden (Benny) McBrien** (Sessiagh, Arney), died 10th Feb. 2001, aged 54 years.

E12-2 [**FLANAGAN** plot with pink granite headstone]. In loving memory of **Joseph Flanagan** (Drumbargy), died Dec. 4, 1979. His brothers: **Frank** died Feb. 20, 1982. **Philip** died Oct. 31, 1984. **Peter** died July 14, 1982. Erected by their sisters, U.S.A.

E12-3 [**CORRIGAN** plot]. In loving memory of **Edward Corrigan** (Drumbargy), died 22nd August 1980. His wife

Transcriptions

Annie died 24th May 1999. And their son **Seamus** died 25th Nov. 2004.

E12-4 [**MAGUIRE** plot]. In loving memory of **Thomas Maguire** (78 Derrin Road, Enniskillen), died 22nd Oct. 1980, aged 82 years. His wife **Agnes** died 4th Nov. 1995, aged 89 years. And their son **Matt** died 29th Nov. 2010, aged 77 years.

E12-5 [**CULLEN** plot]. In loving memory of a devoted wife and mother **Joan Cullen**, died 15th October 2011, aged 63 years. Her husband **John Owen**, a loving father and grandfather, died 23rd March 2018, aged 75 years.

ROW E13

E13-1 [Small marker]. In loving memory of **Johnny McGarry**, died 20th Nov. 1973, aged 80 years.

E13-2 [**BAKER** plot]. In loving memory of **Margaret Baker** (Drumderg), died 12 July 1976. **Bertie Elliott** died 27 March 2001. Erected by the family.

E13-3 [**HASSARD** plot]. In loving memory of **John Hassard** (Carneyhill*), died 30th December 1992, aged 93 years. His wife **Mary Ann** died 18th November 1977, aged 77 years. Their son **Patrick** died 23rd November 1985, aged 48 years.

E13-4 [CORRIGAN plot]. In loving memory of baby **Desmond Corrigan** (Rossdoney), died 25th July 1978.

E13-5 [FEE plot]. In loving memory of **Patrick Fee** (Five Points), died 21st August 1979, aged 63 years. His wife **Mary Jane**, died 3rd February 1984, aged 70 years.

E13-6 [COX plot]. In loving memory of **Leona Cox**, died 3rd June 1979, aged 1 ½ yrs.

E13-7 [**KEARNEY-DRUMM** plot]. Treasured memories of **Michael Kearney**, died 19th August 2006, aged 72 years. Also his granddaughter **Leanne Drumm**, 21st September 1998.

ROW E14

E14-1 [Headstone]. Erected by **Francis O'Brien** in memory of his beloved father **F. O'Brien** who depd. this life Feb. 17th 1840, aged 75 years.

E14-2 [McBRIEN plot]. In loving memory of **John T. McBrien** (Tonyteige*), died 20th November 1976, aged 73 years. His wife **Mary Catherine** died 11th April 1985, aged 79 years.

E14-3 [McBRIEN plot]. In loving memory of **Frank McBrien** (Bellanaleck), died 30th Oct. 1995, aged 59 yrs.

E14-4 [space].

E14-5 [**MacMANUS** partial plot with pedestal marker; note surname spelling differences]. In loving memory of **Ellen MacManus** (*nee* **Cox**), (Derryhowlaght,* Bellanaleck*), died 15th March 1941. Also her husband **James** died 6th July 1952. Interred in St. Patrick's Cemetery, Killesher. [Pedestal]. **Brendan Thomas McManus** died 28th July 1944, aged 5 years.

E14-6 [**FEE-FARMER** plot with two headstones]. 1. In loving memory of **Philip Fee**, died 30th Nov. 1946. His wife **Sarah** died 30th Dec. 1952. Their son **Patrick** died 31st March 1966. Their daughter **Sarah** died 13th July 1974. 2. In loving memory of **Patrick (Paddy) Farmer** (Scaffog), died 22nd December 2009, aged 82 years. His wife **Eileen** died 17th July 2019, aged 88 years. Also remembered babies **Marie**, **Patricia** and **Anna**.

Key to Index of Names

Each person mentioned on the gravestones has been included in the index. This might result in a person being listed more than once in the index because they might have erected a monument for a family member, but were buried under another one. Each person's name has been keyed to his/her location in the cemetery; for example, C2-3, meaning C section, row 2, number 3.

When a woman has been identified as married, her surname has been *italicized*. Where there is uncertainty about ages or dates the numbers have been followed by a ? mark.

Index

Surname	First Names	Death	Loc. #
Baker	Bertie Elliott	2001	E13-2
Baker	Margaret	1976	E13-2
Bannon	Terence	2013	E5-2
Bartley	James	1961	C1-8
Bartley	James Oliver (Jim)	2011	E5-3
Bartley	Margaret Ellen	1974	C1-8
Bartley	Myles	2018	C1-8
Bartley	Myles Patrick	2017	C1-8
Boyle	Brendan	2022	E2-2
Boyle	Declan	2003	E7-6
Boyle	Hannah		C2-9
Boyle	James	1982	C2-5
Boyle	Jane	1981	C2-5
Boyle	Lorraine	1986	C4-20
Boyle	Marie	2011	B4-2
Boyle	Michael	2009	E6-8
Boyle	Noher		C2-9
Boyle			C4-19
Brady	Catherine	1920	A2-23
Brady	John	1889	A2-23
Brady	Winnie	2014	C7-5
Breslin	Jane	1910	B2-5
Breslin	John	1931	B2-5
Breslin	Margaret	1972	B2-5
Brodison			C4-12
Buchholz	Agnes	2022	E2-1
Buchholz	Edward	2021	E2-1

Index

Surname	First Names	Death	Loc. #
Carson	Bridget	1975	C2-5
Carson	William	1959	C2-5
Cassidy	Agnes	1984	A3-5
Cassidy	Anne	1895	C3-3
Cassidy	Bernard	1970	C10-14
Cassidy	Catherine	1912	C10-14
Cassidy	Charlie	2008	C10-14
Cassidy	Edward	1968	A3-5
Cassidy	Henry	1949	B3-5
Cassidy	James	1923	C3-3
Cassidy	James Philip	1938	C3-3
Cassidy	Mary	1934	C3-3
Cassidy	Mary Josephine	1956	C10-14
Cassidy	Patrick	1855	C3-3
Cassidy	Patrick	1933	C3-3
Cassidy	Patrick	1902	C10-14
Cassidy	Phillip	1916	C3-3
Cassidy	Tessie	2002	C10-14
Cassidy	Thomas Gregory	1957	C3-3
Cleary			C1-2
Cole	Jonathan (Johnny)	2018	E4-4
Connors	Patricia	1996	E9-6
Connors	Philip (Phil)	2010	E9-6
Convey	Teresa	1988	A3-14
Convey	William	1989	A3-14
Cooney			A1-15
Cornyn	Bridget	1988	E10-1

Index

Surname	First Names	Death	Loc. #
Cornyn	Murty	2017	E10-1
Cornyn	Murty	2018	E10-1
Corrigan	Anna Christina	1949	C3-5
Corrigan	Anne	1886	C10-1
Corrigan	Annie	1978	C10-20
Corrigan	Annie	1999	E12-3
Corrigan	Bernard	1889	C10-1
Corrigan	Bridget	1899	C10-1
Corrigan	Bridget	1952	C10-20
Corrigan	Desmond	1978	E13-4
Corrigan	Donal	2000	C10-1
Corrigan	Edward	1980	E12-3
Corrigan	Hugh	1973	C3-4
Corrigan	Jane		C8-7
Corrigan	John	1941	C10-20
Corrigan	John	1996	C10-20
Corrigan	John (Sean)	2004	C10-20
Corrigan	Kate	1986	C3-4
Corrigan	Liam	1932	C3-5
Corrigan	Margaret	2002	C3-5
Corrigan	Mary Jacinta	2007	E6-4
Corrigan	Mena	2023	C3-4
Corrigan	Minnie	1986	C10-1
Corrigan	Nathaniel	1845	C10-1
Corrigan	Nathaniel	1955	C10-1
Corrigan	Nathaniel	1953	C10-1
Corrigan	Nathaniel	1995	C10-1

Index

Surname	First Names	Death	Loc. #
Corrigan	Patrick	1957	C3-5
Corrigan	Patrick	1981	C10-3
Corrigan	Patrick (Packie)	2006	C10-1
Corrigan	Philomena	1992	C10-3
Corrigan	Richard	2005	C3-4
Corrigan	Sarah	1947	C10-1
Corrigan	Seamus	2004	E12-3
Corrigan	Teresa	2002	C10-1
Corrigan	Thomas		C10-1
Cox	Alice	1988	A1-8
Cox	Ellen	1922	A1-8
Cox	Ellen	1973	C4-3
Cox	Frances	2009	C4-3
Cox	Jackie	2001	A1-8
Cox	James	1951	C4-3
Cox	John	1968	A1-8
Cox	John	1984	C4-3
Cox	Leona	1979	E13-6
Cox	Mary	2003	A1-8
Cox	Mary Josephine	1930	A1-8
Cox	Patrick	1967	A1-8
Cox	Patrick (Pady)	2005	E6-2
Cox	Philip	1919	A1-8
Cox	Vincent	1956	C4-3
Coyle	Gabriel	1998	E7-1
Creegan	Ellen		C9-2
Creegan	Francis	1921	C9-2

Index

Surname	First Names	Death	Loc. #
Cullen	Aiden	2013	B2-2
Cullen	Andy	2017	E4-3
Cullen	Carmel	2014	B2-2
Cullen	James	1980	B2-2
Cullen	Joan	2011	E12-5
Cullen	John Owen	2018	E12-5
Cullen	Mary Jane	1999	B2-2
Curran	James	1906	C4-8
Curran	John	1914	C4-8
Curran	Mary Jane	1914	C4-8
Curran	Peter		C4-8
Curran	Sarah	1912	C4-8
Curran	William		C4-8
Curry			A2-21
D'Arcy	Angela	1981	A2-3
D'Arcy	Bridget	1927	C10-7
D'Arcy	Gabriel	2011	A2-7
D'Arcy	John Anthony	1972	A2-3
D'Arcy	Josephine	2011	A2-3
D'Arcy	Thomas	1975	A2-3
D'Arcy	Thomas	1912	C10-7
Dolan	Bridget	1979	B10-6
Dolan	John J.	1978	B10-6
Dolan	Lelia	1980	B10-6
Dolan	Susan	1977	C7-1
Donnelly	Jack	1955	D-6
Doogan	Alice	1907	C10-19

Surname	First Names	Death	Loc. #
Doogan	Ann	1926	C10-19
Doogan	Catherine	1883	C7-14
Doogan	Charles Patrick	1906	C7-14
Doogan	Ellen	1914	C7-14
Doogan	John	1917	C7-14
Doogan	Margaret Jane	1919	C10-19
Doogan	Patrick	1853	C7-14
Doogan	Patrick	1915	C10-19
Dray	Mary	1984	C7-1
Drumm	Catherine Jane	1952	C5-2
Drumm	John	1983	E11-4
Drumm	John Thomas	1995	C5-2
Drumm	Kathleen	1999	C5-2
Drumm	Leanne	1998	E13-7
Drumm	Mary	1997	E11-4
Drumm	Philip	1942	C5-2
Farley	Elizabeth	1966	C7-1
Farley	Eugene	1990	C7-1
Farley	John	1958	C7-1
Farley	Patrick Joseph	1993	C7-1
Farmer	Anna		E14-6
Farmer	Bridget	1995	E9-4
Farmer	Eileen	2019	E14-6
Farmer	Jim	1994	E9-4
Farmer	Marie		E14-6
Farmer	Mary	1984	A2-2
Farmer	Patricia		E14-6

Index

Surname	First Names	Death	Loc. #
Farmer	Patrick	1973	A2-2
Farmer	Patrick (Paddy)	2009	E14-6
Farmer	Sean	2008	E6-5
Fee	Mary Jane	1984	E13-5
Fee	Patrick	1979	E13-5
Fee	Patrick	1966	E14-6
Fee	Philip	1946	E14-6
Fee	Sarah	1952	E14-6
Fee	Sarah	1974	E14-6
Fee			B2-2
Flanagan	Frank	1982	E12-2
Flanagan	Joseph	1979	E12-2
Flanagan	Peter	1982	E12-2
Flanagan	Philip	1984	E12-2
Flynn	Jimmy	1967	C3-11
Flynn	John P.	1933	C3-11
Flynn	Mary	1945	C3-11
Foy	Kathleen	2002	C10-22
Gallagher	Christy	1918	B4-3
Gallagher	Elizabeth	1970	B7-3
Gallagher	Felix	1938	B4-3
Gallagher	Hugh	1980	B7-3
Gallagher	Jane	1909	B4-3
Gallagher	Jane	1935	B4-3
Gallagher	John	1869	B4-3
Gallagher	Mary (May)	2013	B7-3
Gallagher	Patrick	1942	B7-3

Index

Surname	First Names	Death	Loc. #
Gallagher	Peggy	1992	B7-3
Gallagher	Thomas	1935	B4-3
Gallagher	Willee	1986	B7-3
Gilbride	Mary	2015	E5-7
Gilheaney	Hugh	2016	E9-5
Gilheaney	James	1964	C7-3
Gilheaney	Jim	1984	E11-5
Gilheaney	John	1995	E9-5
Gilheaney	Mary (Molly)	1980	C7-3
Gilheany	Annie	1969	A1-17
Gilheany	James	1952	A1-17
Gilheany	Kathleen	2006	A1-17
Gilheany	Mairead	1986	A1-17
Gilheany	Thomas	1946	A1-17
Gilheany	Thomas Maurice	1947	A1-17
Gilheany	Walter	1998	A1-17
Gilleece	Anne		C10-6
Gilleece	Hugh		C10-6
Gilleece	John		C10-6
Gilleece	John	1990	C10-6
Gilligan	James	1920	A1-19
Gilligan	Rose	1918	A1-19
Gilligan	Thomas	1922	A1-19
Gilroy	Brigid	1984	C10-9
Gilroy	Denis	1942	C10-9
Gilroy	Denis	1975	C10-9
Gilroy	Kathleen	1977	C10-9

Index

Surname	First Names	Death	Loc. #
Gilroy	Mary Alice	1953	C10-9
Goan	Edward P.		A1-7
Goan			A1-11
Graham	Bridget (Birdie)	2010	A2-20
Graham	Gabriel	2008	A2-20
Graham	Joseph	1972	A2-20
Greene	Catherine	1874	C2-2
Greene	Patrick	1877	C2-2
Greene	William		C2-2
Gunn	John	1931	A1-14
Gunn	Joseph	1905	A1-14
Gunn	Mary Jane	1919	A1-14
Gunn	Rose	1947	A1-14
Hassard	John	1992	E13-3
Hassard	Mary Ann	1977	E13-3
Hassard	Patrick	1985	E13-3
Healy	Catherine	1954	C10-7
Healy	James	1960	C10-7
Henshall	Matthew	2002	E7-5
Herbert	Richard		B5-4
Howe	Annie	1962	B3-8
Howe	Mary Ellen (Cissie)	2004	E6-1
Howe	Thomas	1965	B3-8
Hunt	Eugene	2000	A1-2
Hunt	Eugene Patrick	1977	A1-2
Hunt	Mary Catherine	1977	A1-2
Hunt	Maura	2017	A1-2

Index

Surname	First Names	Death	Loc. #
Judge	Ann Elizabeth	1975	C7-13
Judge	Eileen	1995	A1-23
Judge	Jennifer Marie	1986	C7-13
Judge	John	1971	C7-13
Judge	Mary	2006	C7-13
Judge	Patrick	1990	A1-23
Kearney	Michael	2006	E13-7
Keenan	Ann		C8-8
Keenan	Ann	1863	C8-8
Keenan	Anna Maureen	1999	E7-2
Keenan	Benny		C8-8
Keenan	Bernard		C8-8
Keenan	Betty		C8-8
Keenan	Bridget	1854	B5-5
Keenan	Hugh		B5-5
Keenan	James	1851	B5-5
Keenan	Mary	1897	B5-4
Keenan	Mary		B5-5
Keenan	Mary		C8-8
Keenan	Mary	1863	C8-8
Keenan	Patrick		C8-8
Keenan	Patrick		C8-8
Keenan	Peter		C8-8
Keenan	Phil		C8-8
Keenan	Philip	1856	B5-5
Keenan	Thomas	1895	B5-4
Kelly	Martina	2018	C7-7

Surname	First Names	Death	Loc. #
Kerrin	Manus	1858	C1-10
Kerrin	Michael		C1-10
Kinahan	John Hilary	2019	E4-5
Large	Bernadette	2010	E11-6
Lilly	Denis		C8-6B
Lilly	James John		A2-9
Lilly	John	1838	C8-6B
Lilly	Mary Anne		A2-9
Lilly	Matthew		C8-6B
Lilly	Owen		C8-6B
Lilly	Patt		C8-6B
Lucy	Anna Elizabeth	1944	A2-16
Lucy	Frederick John	2021	A2-16
Lucy	Mary	2014	A2-16
Lucy	William	2000	A2-16
Lunney	Andrew		B1-1
Lunney	Bernard		B1-1
Lunney	Bridget		B1-1
Lunney	Bridget		C10-22
Lunney	John	1938	B1-1
Lunney	John		B1-1
Lunney	John		C10-22
Lunney	John Francis	1984	C10-22
Lunney	Margaret		B1-1
Lunney	Mary		B1-1
Lunney	Mary Anne		B1-1
Lunney	Peter		B1-1

Index

Surname	First Names	Death	Loc. #
Lunney	Terence James	1983	C10-22
Lunney	Thomas		B1-1
Lunney			C4-7
Lunny	James	1979	C1-4
Lunny	Kathleen	2010	C1-4
Lunny	Mary	2013	C8-3
Lunny	Mary Ellen	1975	C1-4
Lunny	Thomas	2000	C8-3
Lynch	Andrew	1939	C10-4
Lynch	Margaret	1953	C10-4
Mackell	Bernard	1910 ?	C4-10
Mackell	Ellen	1865	C4-10
Mackell	Hugh	1915 ?	C4-10
Mackell	Rodger	1847	C4-10
Mackell	Susan	1924	C4-10
Macken	Bridget	1875	C4-5
Macken	Francis	1858	C8-5
Macken	Michael		C4-5
Macken	Neal		C8-5
Macken	Owen	1874	C4-5
Macken	Patrick	1837	C8-5
Macken	Robert	1847	C8-5
Macken	William	1852	C8-5
MacMahon	Eugene	1942	D-5
MacManus	Brenden Thomas	1944	E14-5
MacManus	Ellen	1941	E14-5
MacManus	James	1952	E14-5

Index

Surname	First Names	Death	Loc. #
Magevney	Hugh	1865	C8-1
Magevney	Michael		C8-1
Magevney		1854	C8-1
Maguire	Adam		B9-2
Maguire	Agnes	1995	E12-4
Maguire	Ann	1888	C10-11
Maguire	Ann	1918	C10-11
Maguire	Ann Jane	1979	B10-2
Maguire	Ann Jane	1977	C10-15
Maguire	Catherine	1960	B9-2
Maguire	David		B9-2
Maguire	Ellen		B9-2
Maguire	Ellen Nora	2012	C6-9
Maguire	Gabriel	2021	E3-4
Maguire	Hugh	1970	B10-2
Maguire	James	1909	C10-11
Maguire	James Gerard	2021	B9-2
Maguire	Jane		C10-15
Maguire	John	1919	B4-5
Maguire	John	1953	B9-2
Maguire	John	2004	B10-2
Maguire	John Patrick	1991	C6-9
Maguire	Joseph		C10-15
Maguire	Kathleen	1940	B10-2
Maguire	Lily	1955	B10-2
Maguire	Mary A.		B4-5
Maguire	Matt	2010	E12-4

Index

Surname	First Names	Death	Loc. #
Maguire	Michael	1886	C10-11
Maguire	Pat	1884	C9-14
Maguire	Patrick	1993	B10-6
Maguire	Patrick		C10-15
Maguire	Peter	1922	B4-5
Maguire	Peter	1999	B10-2
Maguire	Rose		B9-2
Maguire	Thelma		B9-2
Maguire	Thomas	1980	E12-4
Maguire	Thomas Alex	2005	C10-12
Maguire	Vincent	2014	E5-4
Martin	Leanne Jennifer	1999	E7-3
Maxwell	Catherine	1905	C4-1
Maxwell	Kathleen	2007	C4-1
McAdam	Margaret	1982	E11-1
McAloon	Andrew		C10-15
McAloon	Ann McManus		C10-15
McAloon	Gary	2020	B4-6
McAloon	Jimmy	2017	E4-2
McAloon	John	1956	B3-7
McAloon	John	1980	B4-6
McAloon	Margaret	1989	A2-17
McAloon	Mary	2019	E4-6
McAloon	Mary Ann	2017	B4-6
McAloon	Michael	1983	B3-7
McAloon	Patricia	1957	B4-6
McAloon	Patrick		C10-15

Index

Surname	First Names	Death	Loc. #
McAloon	Rose	1963	B3-7
McAloon	Sean	2000	A2-17
McAloon	Thomas	1962	A2-17
McAloon	William John		C10-15
McAuley	James	2019	E5-6
McAuley	John	2015	A1-19
McAuley	Mary Ellen	1975	A1-19
McAuley	Patrick	1968	A1-19
McAuley	Sheila	2015	E5-6
McBarron	Anne		A3-15
McBarron	Bridget	1990	A3-15
McBarron	Edward	2011	A3-15
McBarron	Elizabeth		A3-16
McBarron	Hugh	1979	A3-15
McBarron	Hugh	1961	A3-16
McBarron	Hugh Patrick	2006	A3-16
McBarron	John	2020	A3-15
McBarron	Sarah	1976	A3-15
McBarron	Thomas	1950	A3-15
McBrien	Brenden (Benny)	2001	E12-1
McBrien	Bridget	1891	B8-1
McBrien	Catherine	1965	B8-1
McBrien	Eileen	2009	E6-6
McBrien	Francis Gabriel	1934	B8-1
McBrien	Frank	1995	E14-3
McBrien	James	1970	B10-1
McBrien	Jane	1999	B10-1

Index

Surname	First Names	Death	Loc. #
McBrien	John	1975	B8-1
McBrien	John	2012	B8-1
McBrien	John Francis	1939	E12-1
McBrien	John T.	1976	E14-2
McBrien	Mary	1979	E12-1
McBrien	Mary Catherine	1985	E14-2
McBrien	Maura	2013	B8-1
McBrien	Michael	1921	B8-1
McBrien	Patrick	1980	E12-1
McCann			A1-9
McCardle	John		A2-15
McCardle	Margaret Jane	1891	A2-15
McCardle	Mary	1887	A2-15
McConnell	Bernard	1928	A1-21
McConnell	Bernard	1928	B1-3
McConnell	Lizzie	1987	A1-21
McConnell	Lizzie	1987	B1-3
McConnell	Patrick	1972	A1-21
McConnell	Patrick	1972	B1-3
McConnell	Rose	1950	A1-21
McConnell	Rose	1950	B1-3
McConnell	Thomas	1959	A1-21
McConnell	Thomas	1959	B1-3
McConnell			A2-13
McCurrin	Mary		C5-2
McCurrin	Michael	1855	C5-2
McCusker	Brigid	1915	A3-13

116

Index

Surname	First Names	Death	Loc. #
McCusker	Catherine	1886	A3-13
McCusker	Edward	1933	A3-13
McCusker	Thomas	1910	A3-13
McCutcheon	Cassie	1968	A3-7
McCutcheon	Rosealeen	2016	E4-1
McElgunn	John	1944	C10-12
McElgunn	Mary	1954	C10-12
McElgunn	Thomas	1957	C10-12
McElhill	Elizabeth (Lizzie)	2014	B3-3
McElhill	William	1983	B3-3
McElroy	Michael	1964	D-3
McGahey	John	2016	C7-6
McGahey	Kathleen	1979	C7-6
McGahey	Thomas J.	1963	C7-6
McGahey	Thomas J.		C7-6
McGarry	Johnny	1973	E13-5
McGivney	Mary	1849	C2-1
McGivney	Mary	1856	C6-4
McGivney	Michael	1858	C6-4
McGivney	Owen	1892	C2-1
McGivney	Philip		C2-1
McGivney	Philip		C6-4
McGoldbrick	Hugh	1923	A2-23
McGoldbrick	Mary A.		A2-23
McGoldbrick	Peter	1927	A2-23
McGovern	Elizabeth	1954	C9-13
McGovern	Ellen		A3-13

Surname	First Names	Death	Loc. #
McGovern	James	1996	A1-3
McGovern	James	1956	C9-13
McGovern	John	1942	C9-13
McGovern	Mary Veronica	1980	A1-3
McGovern	Michael	1964	C9-13
McGovern	Rose	1967	A1-3
McGovern	Rose Anne	2014	A1-3
McGurn	Eamon	2017	E9-1
McGurn	Gerry	2021	E9-1
McGurn	James	1991	E9-1
McGurn	Margaret	1999	E9-1
McGurn	Sheila	2003	E9-1
McGurrin	Pat		C4-14
McHugh	Alice	2012	E8-6
McHugh	Anne	1930	B9-5
McHugh	Bernard	2002	E8-6
McHugh	Brigid	2003	B9-5
McHugh	Ellen	1919	B9-5
McHugh	Kathleen	1971	B4-5
McHugh	Mary A.	1935	B4-5
McHugh	Peter	1924	B9-5
McHugh	Peter	1969	B9-5
McHugh	Philip	2002	B4-5
McHugh	Renee	1998	B4-5
McKay	Pete	2021	E3-3
McKenzie	Desmond	1999	E7-4
McKenzie	Gerard		E7-4

Index

Surname	First Names	Death	Loc. #
McKenzie	Yvonne	2011	E7-4
McKinney	Margaret	2011	C7-1
McMahon	John	1976	D-2
McManus	Ann Dolan		C10-15
McManus	Brigid	1944	C3-8
McManus	Carmal	1986	C8-6A
McManus	Conor	1951	C3-9
McManus	Daniel		C10-15
McManus	Elizabeth	1874	C9-4
McManus	Helena	1977	A1-2
McManus	Hugh	2020	C8-6A
McManus	James	1938	C3-8
McManus	John	1937	C3-8
McManus	John	1869	C9-4
McManus	Joseph	1861	C9-4
McManus	Kathleen	1994	C3-8
McManus	Margaret	1938	C3-9
McManus	Margaret Mary	1941	C3-9
McManus	Patrick	1951	C3-9
McManus	Patrick J.	1952	D-4
McManus	Patsy	2021	C8-6A
McManus	Paul	1973	C8-6A
McManus	Philip		C9-4
McManus			C1-2
McManus-Maguire	Maggie	1958	B7-1
McNamara	Francis	1978	A2-20
McNamara	Mary Elizabeth	1995	A2-20

Index

Surname	First Names	Death	Loc. #
McTeggart	Elizabeth (Betty)	2009	E6-7
McTeggart	Emily	1995	A2-1
McTeggart	Francis J.	1950	C7-5
McTeggart	Frances Ann	1989	E10-4
McTeggart	Margaret	1942	A1-5
McTeggart	Margaret	1964	A1-5
McTeggart	Owen	1932	A1-5
McTeggart	Owen	1971	C7-7
McTeggart	Owenie	2003	A4-1
McTeggart	Patrick (Paddy)	2023	E6-7
McTeggart	Sarah	1992	C7-7
McTeggart	Thomas	1985	A2-1
McTeggart			C7-3
Meehan	Lisa	2014	E11-3
Meehan	Mark Eugene	1999	E11-3
Meehan	Mary Teresa	2016	E11-3
Meehan	Patrick	1983	E11-3
Monaghan	Bridget	1964	B7-1
Monaghan	Jane	1933	B7-1
Monaghan	Mary	2022	B7-1
Monaghan	Pat	1933	B7-1
Monaghan	Patrick	1970	B7-1
Monaghan	Peter	2005	B7-1
Montgomery	Annie	1953	C3-2
Montgomery	James	1988	B3-2
Montgomery	John	1940	B3-2
Montgomery	John Patrick	1945	C3-2

Surname	First Names	Death	Loc. #
Montgomery	Margaret	1978	C3-2
Montgomery	Mary	1941	B3-2
Montgomery	Mary Ellen	1988	B3-2
Montgomery	Patrick	1993	C3-2
Morris	Daniel (Dan)	2014	E5-5
Murphy	Alice	1944	B2-4
Murphy	Annie	1974	B10-3
Murphy	Charles	1992	E9-2
Murphy	Felix L.	1977	B2-4
Murphy	Irene	1996	E8-2
Murphy	James	1958	B10-3
Murphy	James	2011	B10-3
Murphy	James	1942	C9-12
Murphy	Jane	1928	B2-4
Murphy	Joe	2011	B4-4
Murphy	John	1946	B4-4
Murphy	Mary Anne	1965	C9-12
Murphy	Patricia	2011	B10-3
Murphy	Patrick	1919	B2-4
Murphy	Patrick	2001	B10-3
Murphy	Peter Francis	1948	B2-4
Murphy	Peter Francis	2019	B2-4
Murphy	Rose	1944	B4-4
Murphy	Rose	1982	B4-4
Murphy	Susan	1992	B2-4
Murphy	Teresa	2017	E9-2
Nolan	Bridget	1995	B5-2

Index

Surname	First Names	Death	Loc. #
Nolan	Dympna	2010	B5-2
Nolan	Hugh	1981	C9-10
Nolan	Jody	2013	B5-2
Nolan	John	1963	B5-2
Nolan	Joseph	1974	B5-2
Nolan	Peter	1992	B5-2
O'Brien	Ann	1998	E8-4
O'Brien	Annie	1999	E10-2
O'Brien	F.	1840	E14-1
O'Brien	Francis		E14-1
O'Brien	Hannah		C2-9
O'Brien	Jim	1989	E10-2
O'Connor	Mary Patricia (Pat)	2020	E3-1
O'Lone	Paddy	1977	B3-3
O'Neal	Catherine	1852	C4-15
O'Neal	Patrick		C4-15
O'Prey	Delia	1972	A2-21
O'Prey	John	1991	C3-11
O'Prey	Mary Jane	2003	C3-11
O'Prey	Patrick	1945	A2-21
O'Prey	Thomas Patrick	2002	A2-21
Owens	Andrew	1956	C1-6
Owens	Andrew	2001	C1-7
Owens	Anna	2003	C1-7
Owens	Anne	1927	C6-5
Owens	Annie		A2-8
Owens	Annie	1939	C6-4

122

Index

Surname	First Names	Death	Loc. #
Owens	Bridget	1852	C6-5
Owens	Bridget	2002	E8-1
Owens	Cassie		A2-8
Owens	Damien	1980	C6-4
Owens	Ellen	1973	C1-6
Owens	Francis	1958	C1-7
Owens	Francis	2020	E3-2
Owens	Francis Thomas	1942	C6-4
Owens	Helen Cecilia		C6-5
Owens	Hugh Patrick	1986	C6-4
Owens	James	1996	E8-1
Owens	Jamesie		A2-8
Owens	John		C6-5
Owens	John F. (Sean)	2003	E8-7
Owens	Malachy	2020	E8-7
Owens	Margaret		C6-5
Owens	Mary		C6-5
Owens	Mary T.	2010	C1-6
Owens	Maurice	1853	C6-5
Owens	Nathaniel	1868	C6-5
Owens	Philip	2001	C1-6
Owens	Philip	1965	C6-5
Owens	Philip	2000	C6-5
Owens	Rita	2018	E8-7
Owens	Rose Ann	1998	C6-4
Owens	Rosealeen	2015	E5-8
Owens	T.P.	2019	E5-8

Index

Surname	First Names	Death	Loc. #
Owens	Tom	1944	C6-4
Packenham	Elizabeth	1999	A3-7
Packenham	Patrick	1969	A3-7
Parr	Rose Philomena	2009	A2-17
Power	Mary Ellen	2019	A1-23
Quigley	Bernard (Bertie)	1995	E11-6
Quigley	Bridget	1932	C6-9
Quigley	Bridget	2018	E10-3
Quigley	Eddie	2001	E10-3
Quigley	Eugene	1973	C7-12
Quigley	Francis	1928	C7-12
Quigley	James	1938	C6-9
Quigley	Josephine	1986	C7-12
Quigley	Mary Anne	1957	C7-12
Quigley	Noel	1973	C7-12
Quigley	Patrick	1988	E11-6
Quigley	William John	1989	E10-3
Quigley	Winifred	1987	E11-6
Quinn	Annie Eleanor	2010	A1-6
Quinn	Frank		A2-4
Quinn	Frank	1991	A3-1
Quinn	Hugh	1966	A1-6
Quinn	John	1970	A3-5
Quinn	John Patrick	2010	E8-5
Quinn	Kathleen	1985	A3-1
Quinn	Margaret		A2-4
Quinn	Mary A.	1906	A3-13

Index

Surname	First Names	Death	Loc. #
Quinn	Mary Anne	1958	A3-5
Quinn	Sarah	1956	A1-6
Quinn	Theresa	1999	E8-5
Reihill	Anne	1958	C8-3
Reihill	Joseph	1977	C8-3
Reihill	Patrick	1976	C8-3
Riley	Elizabeth M.		C10-15
Robinson	Bridget	1974	C10-7
Robinson	James	1975	C10-7
Rooney	Margaret	1943	C6-9
Sheridan	Patrick	1951	C7-9
Sheridan	Sarah	1975	C7-9
Sherrin	Catherine	1994	E9-3
Slavin	Mary	1887	C10-1
Slevin	Catherine	1950	A2-11
Slevin	Hugh	1923	A2-11
Slevin	Hugh	1983	A2-11
Slevin	Joseph	1948	A2-11
Slevin	Susan	1927	A2-11
Slowey	Kevin	1994	D-1
Smyth	Frances	1986	A1-11
Smyth	John	1981	A1-11
Snow	Mary	1977	C10-17
Snow	Matthew	1966	C10-17
Spence	Laura	2012	E5-1
Thompson	Eithne Mary	2005	E6-3
Timoney	Cassie Jane	1953	C3-7

Index

Surname	First Names	Death	Loc. #
Timoney	James		C3-7
Timoney	Jimmy	1997	C3-7
Timoney	John	1951	C3-7
Timoney	John	1880	C2-7
Timoney	John Patrick	1978	C3-7
Timoney	Josephine		C2-7
Timoney	Margaret	1875	C3-7
Timoney	Mary	1922	B8-1
Timoney	Patrick	1864	C3-7
Ward	Agnes	2008	E8-3
Ward	Patrick	1996	E8-3
Woodcock	Kate	1969	A3-4
Woodcock	Willie	1978	A3-4

Old and New Irish Genealogy Series Titles

County Antrim

Racavan Burying Ground, Racavan Parish; 895 names. ISBN 978-1-927357-66-8. 2020

County Donegal

Finner Cemetery, Bundoran, Inishmacsaint Parish; 1008 names from Donegal and Leitrim. ISBN 978-1-927357-34-7. 2012

St. Anne's Church of Ireland Cemetery, Ballyshannon, Kilbarron Parish; 1217 names. ISBN 978-1-927357-52-1. 2016

County Fermanagh

Aghalurcher Parish

Holy Cross Roman Catholic Cemetery, Lisnaskea; 1240 names. ISBN 978-1-927357-80-4. 2025

Holy Trinity Church of Ireland Cemetery, Lisnaskea; 1296 names. ISBN 978-1-927357-79-8. 2025

Maguiresbridge Church of Ireland Cemetery; 516 names. ISBN 978-1-927357-40-8. 2014

Maguiresbridge Methodist Cemetery; 343 names. ISBN 978-1-927357-41-5. 2014

Maguiresbridge Presbyterian Cemetery; 206 names. ISBN 978-1-927357-42-2. 2014

St. Mary's Roman Catholic Cemetery, Maguiresbridge; 1296 names. ISBN 978-1-927357-68-2. 2020

Aghavea Parish

A Comprehensive Index of the Aghavea Church of Ireland Parish Registers, 1815-1912; over 8300 entries from Aghavea and Aghalurcher parishes. ISBN 978-1-927357-61-3. 2018

Aghavea Church of Ireland Cemetery; 1118 names. ISBN 978-1-927357-38-5. 2013

St. Mary's Roman Catholic Churchyard and Carrickyheenan Road Cemetery, Brookeborough; 692 names. ISBN 978-1-927357-65-1. 2019

Irish Genealogy Series

Boho Parish

Boho Church of Ireland Parish Register; 572 entries ISBN 978-0-9781764-2-6. 2006

Boho Church of Ireland Cemetery; 245 names from Fermanagh and Cavan. ISBN 978-0-9781764-6-4. 2008

St. Faber's Roman Catholic Cemetery; 757 names. ISBN 978-1-927357-01-09. 2011

Cleenish Parish

A Comprehensive Index of the Bellanaleck Church of Ireland Parish Registers (1845-1912); over 742 entries from Fermanagh and Cavan. (CD-ROM) ISBN 978-1-927357-49-1. 2015

Bellanaleck Church of Ireland Cemetery; 624 names. ISBN 978-0-9812063-7-0. 2011

Lisbellaw Church of Ireland Churchyard; 431 names. ISBN 978-1-927357-10-1. 2012

Lisbellaw Presbyterian Cemetery; 110 names. ISBN 978-1-927357-39-2. 2013

Mullaghdun Church of Ireland Cemetery; 354 names. ISBN 978-0-9812063-6-3. 2011

Irish Genealogy Series

A Comprehensive Index of the Mullaghdun Church of Ireland Cleenish Parish Registers (1819-1912); over 2770 entries from Fermanagh and Cavan. ISBN 978-1-927357-35-4. 2013

St. Joseph's Roman Catholic Cemetery, Mullaghdun; 414 names. ISBN 978-1-927357-13-2. 2012

St. Patrick's Holy Well Cemetery, Belcoo; 784 names. ISBN 978-1-927357-58-3. 2017

Templerushin (Holy Well) Graveyard, Belcoo; 82 names ISBN 978-1-927357-57-6. 2017

St. Mary's Catholic Cemetery, Arney; 688 names. ISBN 978-1-927357-78-1. 2025

Derrybrusk Parish

St. Michael's Church of Ireland Cemetery; 393 names. ISBN 978-1-927357-59-0. 2018

Devenish Parish

A Comprehensive Index of the Devenish Church of Ireland Parish Registers; over 6300 entries. ISBN 978-0-9812063-9-4. 2011

Irish Genealogy Series

St. Patrick's Roman Catholic Cemetery, Derrygonnelly; 713 names. ISBN 978-0-9812063-2-5. 2010

Garrison Church of Ireland Cemetery; 304 names from Fermanagh, Leitrim, and Donegal. ISBN 978-0-9781764-7-1. 2008

St. Molaise Church of Ireland Cemetery, Monea; 905 names. ISBN 978-1-927357-00-2. 2012

Monea Roman Catholic Cemetery; 315 names. ISBN 978-0-9869627-4-5. 2011

Drumkeeran Parish

Colaghty Church of Ireland and Tirwinny Methodist Cemeteries; 615 names. ISBN 978-1-927357-75-0. 2025

Tubrid Church of Ireland Graveyard; updated. 575 names. ISBN 978-1-927357-77-4. 2025

Enniskillen Parish

Enniskillen Poor Law Union, Outdoor Relief Register Index: 1847-1899; about 3000 entries from Fermanagh, Tyrone and Cavan. ISBN 978-0-9781764-1-9. 2009

Irish Genealogy Series

Memorials in the Enniskillen Presbyterian Church; 110 names. ISBN 978-1-927357-67-5. 2020

Mount Lourdes Convent Cemetery, Enniskillen; over 2000 names. ISBN 978-1-927357-81-1. 2025

Inishmacsaint Parish

A Comprehensive Index to the Inishmacsaint Church of Ireland Parish Registers, Counties Fermanagh and Donegal (1800-1912); contains over 12,000 entries for Fermanagh, Donegal and Leitrim. ISBN 978-1-927357-55-2. 2016

Benmore Church of Ireland Cemetery; 613 names. ISBN 978-0-9781764-4-0. 2012

Old Derrygonnelly Churchyard; 332 names. ISBN 978-0-9781764-8-8. 2009

Garrison Roman Catholic Cemetery; 1050 names. ISBN 978-0-9812063-0-1. 2009

Slavin Church of Ireland Cemetery; 209 names from Fermanagh and Donegal. ISBN 978-1-927357-19-4. 2012

Three Old Inishmacsaint Parish Graveyards: Inishmacsaint Island, Carrick and Old Slavin; 129 names. ISBN 978-0-9869627-1-4. 2011

Irish Genealogy Series

St. John the Baptist Roman Catholic Cemetery; 595 names. ISBN 978-1-927357-07-01. 2012

Magheracross Parish

Sydare Methodist Cemetery; 1247 names from Fermanagh, Tyrone and Donegal. ISBN 978-0-9781764-9-5. 2008

Two Magheracross Parish Burial Grounds: Old Magheracross Graveyard and the Ballina-mallard Church of Ireland Churchyard; 588 names from Fermanagh and Tyrone. ISBN 978-0-9812063-4-9. 2010

Magheraculmoney Parish

A Comprehensive Index of the St. Mary's Ardess Church of Ireland, Magheraculmoney Parish Registers, County Fermanagh, 1763-1918; 15,630 entries for Fermanagh and Tyrone. ISBN 978-1-927357-71-2. 2021

Edenclaw Catholic Cemetery, Ederney; 579 names. ISBN 978-1-927357-76-7. 2025

Rossorry Parish

Rossorry Parish Cemeteries; 1250 names. ISBN 978-0-9781764-0-2. 2009

Trory Parish

Killadeas Church of Ireland Cemetery; 283 names. ISBN 978-1-927357-04-0. 2012

St. Michael's Church of Ireland Cemetery; 320 names. ISBN 978-0-9812063-1-8. 2009

County Leitrim

Kiltyclogher Church of Ireland Churchyard, Cloonclare Parish; 20 names from Leitrim and Fermanagh. ISBN 978-1-927357-70-5. 2020

Old Rossinver Graveyard, Rossinver Parish; 1073 names from Leitrim and Fermanagh. ISBN 978-1-927357-50-7. 2016

Irish Genealogy Series

County Tyrone

St. John's Church of Ireland Churchyard, Fivemiletown, Clogher Parish; 1379 names from Tyrone and Fermanagh. ISBN 978-1-927357-16-3. 2012

St. Joseph's Catholic Cemetery, Fivemiletown, Clogher Parish; 432 names. (in production).

County Wicklow

Old Kilmurry Roman Catholic Cemetery, Newcastle Parish; 187 names. ISBN 978-1-927357-37-8. 2013

CONTACT:

For information on where you can obtain any of the preceding titles contact KinFolk Finders by email or by phone.

Email: kinfolkfinders154@gmail.com

Phone: 1-519-294-0728.

www.ingramcontent.com/pod-product-compliance
Lightning Source LLC
Chambersburg PA
CBHW061248230426
43663CB00021B/2940